KEEP ON,
KEEPIN' ON!

To Glynna,
My Panera friend —
Always —
Keep On Keepin On!
Alan

KEEP ON, KEEPIN' ON!

It's Not Where We Start,
It's Where We Finish!

C. Alan Axley

Keep On, Keepin' On! / C. Alan Axley

ISBN: 978-0-578-54-54194-5

DEDICATION

I dedicate this book to my family, friends, and business relationships that I have been fortunate enough to develop over the years.

I'm so thankful for my sons, Steve and Tim, who have given me so much joy as they excel in their life journey. I thank Carol Axley for having partnered as my wife while meandering our way through the ups and downs of raising a family. I thank my brother, Tom, for being my childhood teammate, as we overcame family difficulties on our paths to adulthood.

To my grandchildren, John, Sophie, and Audrey. As time progresses, and new generations emerge, I feel it's important to understand some of the history of earlier generations. Hopefully, as they grow and mature, they may learn from the failures and successes of those that came before them.

Lastly, to my best friend and wife, Stacey, I feel so fortunate to have you as my teammate, at this time in my life. A verse from the famous song, Desperado, by the Eagles rings true for me; "You Better Let Somebody Love You, Before It's Too, Late! I opened my heart, and I'm so happy that I did.
I feel blessed.

CONTENTS

ACKNOWLEDGMENTS

In becoming a first-time author, I would like to acknowledge those who helped me organize the structure and core ingredients it took to tell my story.

The following individuals gave me help and encouragement during the process of writing a book.

I thank Tracy Atkins of "The Book Makers" for the professional layout and formatting of the interior of my book.

The first thing that catches your eye when looking at a book is the cover. I thank Tanja Prokop with "Book Cover World" for the unique graphic design for my book cover

I thank my friend Marine General John Admire, a military hero, an author, and my high school teammate. I can't thank John enough for his guidance and expertise in helping me to express my thoughts on paper.

I thank my wife, Stacey, for her input and helping to edit copy and restore old family photographs, which is a significant part of the story.

Lastly, thanks to the ones who were the guinea pigs that read rough drafts, and gave me their honest input, good and bad.

FORWARD

Alan Axley has done what most of us only talk or dream about doing. He has dared to bare his heart and soul in writing his story describing his life's path. Because of time, our history is sometimes forgotten or has, inadvertently, disappeared. Many of us have probably wished we had asked our parents or grandparents to tell us their stories, to help us learn more about our family's past.

Alan and I have been friends for over fifty years, since our high school days. We share a common blue-collar background of poverty and hard times. He writes affectionately and nostalgically of his Grandma Box and her critical role in his life. He writes passionately and respectfully about his relationships, the struggles of his single-parent mother, and of forgiving his absentee-father. He writes about Coach Bill Allen, our high school coach, who mentored and blessed us with his leadership and fatherly advice. As a senior in high school, I captained our team and Alan, a sophomore, sat on the bench. Later, Alan played at the University of Oklahoma, while I sat proudly in the bleachers and cheered for him.

Interestingly, and typically Alan, his family story is more about those who have inspired and influenced his life than it is about him. Alan was an All-State basketball player at Tulsa Webster High School who earned a coveted scholarship to the University of Oklahoma. He became a successful and respected sales achiever, business executive, and corporate leader. While achieving success in his professional life, his most cherished times and memories are those of sports activities, business partnerships, and personal experiences he shared with his sons. As in life, Alan's modesty is revealed as he shares more thoughts about his shortcomings and mistakes than his successes.

While I served in three wars and five combat tours as an Infantry Marine, Alan is the true hero for the battle he fought and won against Cancer. Alan's goal was to write a truthful and heartfelt story for his family and friends. He's done exactly that. In our talks about writing, we agreed that he was no Shakespeare, but in turn, we also agreed Shakespeare never dunked a basketball. That's Alan's game... and Alan's story has game!

General John Admire, U.S. Marines

INTRODUCTION

I never thought I'd ever write a book. I remember making decent grades in English and Literature classes. However, my handwriting was not as good as I would have liked. I was just happy that I was adequate enough to make decent grades with any writing assignment given to me. In some of my written work, letters in a word would be reversed. I didn't know till later in life that I might have had a slight case of dyslexia.

This book is not going to be a great work of art or include eloquent verbiage, but hopefully, I will be able to convey some of my many memories and personal life lessons to pass on to my friends, acquaintances, and loved ones.

As I've been busy composing my memoir, I've discovered something very unexpected. I found that in writing and recalling life experiences, you learn much more about yourself and, especially, how difficult it is to turn your feelings into words.

In starting my book, I ran across a quote from Octavia Spencer, where she said, *"the hardest thing about writing, for me, is facing the blank page!*

I'm staring at a blank page...so, here goes!

SECTION ONE
THE JOURNEY

1

RETIREMENT

*"The Trouble With Retirement Is That
You Never Get A Day Off!"*
Abe Lemons…College Basketball Coach

So, this is it. This is what it feels like?

December 31, 2015, was a day that I thought I'd never have to face. That's the day I formally retired. Truth be known, I probably retired a couple of years earlier because I didn't work as hard as in the past. I guess I didn't have the "fire in the belly" it takes to be in business and sales, anymore.

It's hard for me to write about my feelings on the subject of retirement. I've always told everyone that asked, or every time I watched others retire, that "I'll Never Retire!" Well, regardless, it's here. I'm not excited about it, but at the same time, I'm not really sad. I do feel as though I need to be doing something, and I'm almost feeling guilty about not working. I want to emphasize almost! As you can tell by my mixed emotions, I'm not sure how I feel?

People keep asking me what I'm going to do with my time, and I act like I know by responding with vague answers. When the conversation keeps lending itself to retirement, I come up with the same jargon that I've heard others verbalize when asked the question? I reply as if I'm confident with phrases such as, I'll travel, I'll spend time with the family, I'll see my grandkids more often, I'll volunteer to help others, or I'll add more hobbies to my now full repertoire.

After much thought, I finally decided that I needed to move toward a new goal. So, I'm writing a memoir. I can honestly say that I had mixed feelings of revisiting the road map of my life, while now in my early 70's.

At first, it was a challenge for me to revisit my past and share my experiences with family and friends. I had to ask myself a question? "Alan, why do you think you are so important that you want to share your life long experiences with others? Randomly, I found an answer to that question from two quotes by Steve Jobs, the founder of Apple. The first jewel that caught my eye was, "We're Here To Put A Dent In The Universe. Otherwise, Why Else Even Be Here?" With that, I thought to myself, what was my Dent? Am I leaving a "footprint" on planet earth? Memories of family experiences, relationships, personal challenges, and the various obstacles I overcame, started to emerge.

Being that I was never an author or even an average student of journalism, I was unsure of creating a book in which I would convert my stories and feelings into words. I guess I was a little insecure and doubted if I was up to the challenge. Finally, the second quote by Jobs brought back my competitiveness when he said, "Life can be much broader once you discover one simple fact--everything around you that you call life was made up by people that were no smarter than you!" With those words, my confidence began to build toward the challenge ahead.

I can honestly say that I have mixed feelings of revisiting the road map of my life. In one way, it passed very quickly, but when I started to recall events or memories, it seemed like it took a long time to amass those experiences.

Eventually, through life's ups and downs, I hope to find more opportunities to contribute to the universe, in positive ways. In recalling events of the past, there are things I may have done right, if even by accident. There are also many things I wish I'd done differently.

KEEP ON, KEEPIN' ON!

Whatever the path that I took and that I followed, I want my friends and relatives to know that it was my good or bad "choices" that brought me to this point in my life. As Dr. Wayne Dyer put it, "Your life is a sum total of the choices you've made!" I'm still making choices, even though the choices I make today seem to be much easier and smarter than they were when I was younger.

2

SHACK LIFE

"Where You Start In Life
Is Not As Important as Where You Finish"
Zig Ziglar…Motivational Speaker/Author

My early childhood memories centered around my time with my Grandma Axley Box and life in the Shack. The Shack was Grandma Box's old two-room house made of worn and weathered wood.

I had never known my Grandpa Axley, who had passed away before I was born, at the age of thirty-six.

Mr. Box, her second husband, was much older and frail, so he wasn't much help, physically. Because of Mr. Box's age, Grandma Box seemed to be in charge of all chores, inside and out. Money was tight, and Grandma did what many had to do in 1940s small rural communities, and that was to buy groceries by "putting them on the bill." I guess you could say it was a simple form of today's credit cards. Being that Bixby was a small community, the store owner knew you by your first name. He trusted that you'd pay when your employer paid you or, for older adults like Mr. Box, when your "old age pension" of ninety dollars a month came in the mail.

If you hadn't paid your grocery bill at the end of the month, the store owner would prefer not to sell you anything further, until the account was clear. Grandma would walk to town, which was a couple of blocks away, to shop for our necessities such as, flour, shortening (lard), baking powder, beans, and sugar. She had no modern refrigerator, so the items she bought at the store were things that didn't need to be kept cold.

There wasn't any refrigeration in the little grocery store, so she bought fresh butter and milk from a farmer, or traded for what was needed. She grew vegetables, so we had a variety of what we needed from her a small garden. What refrigeration we had for eggs and poultry was from her wooden "icebox." The iceman delivered a 25 lb. chunk of ice, periodically, by using his ice tongs. He'd place the square chunk of ice into the top of the icebox to help keep things cool in the bottom. There was a drain pan below the box to collect water as the ice melted, which was about two days, at the most.

Recently, I found an old icebox at an antique store in Tulsa, just like the one we had in the Shack. I refinished it and set it in the kitchen of my house. I also acquired an artist rendering of an ice delivery truck, pulled by a horse and buggy, to deliver the ice to patrons. They are constant reminders of those days in the Shack.

Some of the past is so vivid that I can almost see or smell the surroundings. In remembering my time with Grandma in the Shack, I recall the antique table covered in cheap plastic that sat in the room that was considered the kitchen. I loved eating old fashion pinto beans, cornbread, and fried potatoes that she'd just cooked on a cast-iron wood-burning stove.

I didn't wear shoes in the summer, so when walking and playing on worn-out wood floors, there would be splinters that could penetrate my bare feet. The inner walls of the small dwelling were made up of pieces from old cardboard boxes. The tin roof was so loud when it rained or sleeted, that you'd thought it was like a thousand hammers hitting it, all at once.

Because of the heat in the summer, we had to keep the windows wide open. There were no screens on the windows, which allowed many outside pests to come inside freely. Flies were everywhere, especially in the kitchen. Being a kid and finding ways to entertain myself, I used to see how many flies I could hit with a worn-out metal flyswatter, all at once. It became a game for me. It wouldn't be so funny today.

In the so-called living room or front room, there was a potbellied stove sitting in the center of the small room, for heating in the winter. The coal and woodpile, used for fuel, was about twenty-five yards outside the kitchen door. At a young age, I was barely able to carry a full bucket of coal into the house. Once you placed the coal into the stove, you'd add splintered wood or kindling, to light a small fire to ignite the coal. The stove eventually got white-hot. You didn't want to get to close to it, because there was always the danger of severe burns if you accidentally came in contact with it.

The outdoor toilet was not a pretty sight. People of the city used to make jokes about the weathered and poorly built out-houses, but many in the rural areas could not afford an indoor toilet or septic tanks. In tough times, toilet paper was in short supply and expensive. To make up for that, we'd tear out pages from a Sears's catalog, or other old magazines that been thrown away by others, to "finish your business." I guess you do what you have to do. We did!

We didn't have much furniture and what we did have was worn and dilapidated. In the living room, there was an old couch on one side of the room. In the same room, you could enter the Shack through the front door, where there was a small bed on each side of the entrance. There was a dresser across from the couch before you entered the next room, which was the kitchen. With no electricity, in the evening, Grandma Box would light a flame in one coal-oil lamp that sat on the living room dresser, to give us light till we went to bed. It was a treat for me, as I looked forward to blowing out the flame before bedtime.

On the other side of the house from the woodpile and mound of coal, was the fenced chicken yard. It was a necessity to have a rooster and chickens for our food and eggs. Yes, when we needed food, we'd sacrifice a hen by "wringing its neck." It was not pretty seeing someone sacrifice a chicken, but there were no going to the grocery stores for pre-packaged chicken, as today. Beef was not an option, as the cost was too high. Most farmers or ranchers kept their meat or sold it to restaurants for those who could afford it.

We had water from an outdoor well that was located deep underground. We carried the water for drinking, cooking, and washing our face and hands into the house with a small water bucket. To get the water out of the ground, we used an iron hand pump. We'd "prime the pump" by adding a small amount of water into the top of the pump. By rigorously pushing and pulling the handle hard, it would start water flowing from a freshwater well that was ten to fifteen feet below ground level.

Those early years were special to me in Bixby, but the one event that stands out for me in the late 1940's was the "Green Corn Festival."

Bixby was located in an agricultural area, in which the main cash crop was corn, which flourished on the Arkansas River bottom that surrounded the town. In the early summer, and all around the fertile farmland, the prized fields of corn were sold and exported to major cities, such as Dallas and Kansas City. Because of the importance of the crop to the community, every summer the town celebrated it's Green Corn Festival, which took place over a long weekend, in early June.

The center of the celebration was the town square, where they proudly displayed the American flag. The boxing ring stage was for various types of community interaction and entertainment. On the stage, you would see everything from local Western Swing Bands, Country Dancing, Amateur Talent Shows, Semi-Pro Wrestling, Kids Boxing Matches, and various contests to keep everyone entertained. For the young kids, there was a small park down the street with a carnival that included rides and games.

Every year at the festival, there was a drawing for a grand prize. The grand prize, when I was there in the late forties, was a new nineteen-inch black and white table model television set, which included a rabbit ear antenna. At the time, there were only two television channels for viewing, and programming was simple. The television programming consisted of the local news, a few comedy shows, western swings bands, religious shows, and a kid's show called, Howdy Doody.

On the last Saturday night of the festival, there would be a drawing for the television. As I placed my grandma's entry into a large chicken wired container, everyone waited anxiously for the winning ticket to be selected. "Rosie Box," they called! Yes, my grandma had won a television. Knowing that Rosie was poor and didn't have money for extravagant purchases, everyone was excited for her. However, almost immediately, the atmosphere went from excitement to some nervous apprehension. Everyone began to realize that Rosie did not have electricity!

After the excitement started to die down, a businessman and the guy who owned the Shack, volunteered to take the small television home for Grandma. With financial help from the businessman, the next day an electric light pole was installed on the street that was close to the Shack. The workers for the utility company ran an electrical line from the road to the small dwelling so that Rosie could watch her new technological appliance. I was not sure about Grandma, but I was ecstatic!

We could now plug the television into an extension cord hanging from the ceiling in the front room, to watch television shows. As well, the small electric line would also hold one light bulb. With that, we no longer had to depend, solely, on lighting from a coal-oil lamp in the evening hours, before bed.

In 2019, the Green Corn Festival is still alive and well in Bixby, Oklahoma. That community celebration brings back great memories.

My early life with Grandma in the Shack was just the beginning for me. I cherished and loved those early years with Rosie Box and my life with her. But, I also know that even at that early age, I had visions of electric lights, indoor toilets, water faucets, and a house on a hill that was out of a flood zone.

It would take a while, but my dreams would get even bigger!

3

PERSEVERE

"In the middle of difficulty,
lies opportunity."
Albert Einstein…Physicist

I don't recall my birth father, Cecil Axley, being around much at an early age. My first memories of my mom were of her being married to Tommy Johnston, my brother's father. Mom said that she and Tommy were married in Oklahoma City on their way to San Diego, where my brother was born. Later on, they relocated to Amarillo, Texas, where I joined them, as I began my education in the first grade.

I'd visited Grandma Box every summer during my first three school years, but as I visited her after that third year in school, my mom's second marriage was becoming untangled. Mom and my brother would move back to Tulsa, later that summer, where I would join them for good. In the fall, my brother and I enrolled in an elementary school on the north side of Tulsa, as we began to become a little more stable, for a short time.

During the next year, my father, Cecil, started showing up and dating my mom, more and more. Subsequently, during that year, they got back together, and we all moved from a one-room apartment to a larger apartment in the same rundown area. Life started to become a little more reliable for my brother and me, but there were still obstacles that Cecil had not overcome. His drinking always kept us all unnerved. We never knew if he was going to be home, or out on a binge. I had hoped that their second marriage would become a little more stable for us, but that would not be the case.

Hard liquor was illegal in Oklahoma till the late 1950's, so around Tulsa and eastern Oklahoma, you could find many whiskey stills that manufactured illegal "moonshine liquor." Liquor was also brought illegally into Oklahoma from out of state. Cecil became one of those who smuggled whiskey. Those individuals driving automobiles with hidden illegal liquor on the highway and across state lines were called "moonshine runners."

The whiskey bootlegger, or the distributor in Tulsa, owned a 1949 Studebaker automobile that had two gas tanks. Cecil drove the car for the boss, in which one tank contained gasoline, and the other was filled with the illegal liquor. There was a movie made in 1958 starring Robert Mitchum called, "Thunder Road." It depicted the dangers that Cecil faced in his job. Moonshine runners could not only be put in prison or risk being shot by police, but other competitive bootleggers were a danger to them, as well.

I remember times when Cecil would come home with a fist full of cash. A meeting was then set up with his boss to deliver the profits from the illegal liquor transaction. Mom would tell Cecil that he deserved a great deal of that money for the risk that he was taking in going to jail. But, from what I heard in the conversations, he never skimmed money on the payout. He handed all of the cash over to his bootlegger distributor, who then paid him what was previously negotiated, between the two of them.

After a few months, Mom convinced Cecil to leave the illegal liquor business and get a regular job. He now had a mundane job delivering eggs and groceries for a Tulsa wholesale food company, to various restaurants and grocery stores. It was not as exciting, but it also wasn't a life and death situation for every trip or delivery he'd make.

With mom working as a waitress and Cecil having a regular job, we moved out of an apartment to a rental house on the Westside of Tulsa. It was our first taste of a blue-collar working community of homeowners, rather than cheap apartments. It would be a part of town that my brother and I would grow to love. However, Cecil's job with the food company didn't last long. Tommy and I would attend a new school for only about half a year at Robertson Elementary School, before moving again.

Cecil had always felt at home being a laborer on the farm. Louis Baker, a large farm owner who had hired him in the past, offered him a job. They would love having Cecil back because he was a personable and strong-bodied guy, who was an experienced farm worker. Having grown up in Bixby, he knew those who owned farms and was comfortable being a farm laborer, or driving a tractor to plant and harvest those rich vegetables.

Mr. Baker offered Cecil and us a free place to live. It was a small farmhouse that sat in the middle of a large vegetable farm near Leonard, Oklahoma. Leonard was a small farming community about six miles south of Bixby. When one would arrive at Leonard while driving on the highway, there was only a service station, a café, and a few houses on each side of the road. Where we would live was a few miles off the highway toward the fertile farmland of the Arkansas River bottom. To me, it seemed like it was out in the middle of nowhere. It was definitely off the beaten path.

Modern conveniences that I had recently gotten accustomed to in a city were limited. The house we moved in to had no running water. We only a hand pump for well water, that was located right outside the kitchen door. About twenty yards away, there was an outdoor toilet. To the left of that, and farther away, was a small barn and chicken house with live chickens for food and eggs. It was just as it was with my grandma, in the Shack.

Tommy and I attended Leonard school, a small country school with classes for first through eighth grade. Many grades had two to three of those classes in the same room and were taught by one teacher. The sturdy native stone building had a large common area with a huge potbellied stove to, supposedly, carry heat to the surrounding classrooms.

Mom still worked in Tulsa as a waitress and ran a café in Sand Springs, a small suburb of Tulsa. She commuted from Sand Springs to Leonard every Monday through Saturday. In the winter, it would be dark driving back home on those small two-lane country roads from Tulsa to Leonard. We still teased mom, later in life, about her story of seeing a flying saucer on her drive home one night from Tulsa. She described a flash of light roaring across the sky and then, in a fast decent, a beam of light quickly screamed across her windshield. She almost wrecked her car when she noticed that the bright light moved back up into the sky and followed her home. Till the day she died, she was adamant that there were flying saucers from other planets, in our midst. As well, she was a great believer in the zodiac signs and the alignment of the stars, to tell her future. Tom and I laughed with her, many times when recalling those extraterrestrial stories.

I can say that Tommy and I were bored when we were out of school in the summer, at Leonard. Mom could sense we were not happy but, eventually, we would talk her into letting us play little league baseball in Tulsa. She decided to let us try out for a baseball team with former classmates from Robertson Elementary, the last school we had attended in Tulsa. Mom began to take us to our Aunt Cora's in the daytime and then pick us up after work and baseball practice, for our trip back to Leonard. By doing that, it gave us much wanted contacts back in Tulsa. We were excited and found that being on a team with uniforms and teammates our age, made us miss city life, more and more.

With summer winding down, there would be a significant change coming for us. Like I said, Cecil's boss liked him because he was a hard-working farmhand, but Cecil was still a drinker and partier after a week of work. When he got back home to Leonard and Bixby, where he grew up, he tended to work hard from Monday till payday on Friday. However, sometimes after work on Friday and being paid in cash, Cecil would go out drinking at bars and may not be back home till Sunday. He and Mom got into fights because of his actions and lack of responsibility. She would cuss, call him a drunk, and torment him to try to make him feel guilty, which didn't seem to work. Sitting on the couch with a hangover, I can remember him just sitting there and listening until he couldn't take any more. Cecil would say to her in a firm voice, "Shut up and go to bed!" She wouldn't quit ranting and kept taunting him, so his voice would get louder and more forceful, as he'd repeat, "Shut up and go to bed!" After a while, she'd tone down. My brother and I were always fearful that a verbal argument would turn physical, but thankfully, it was almost always just loud cursing and screaming. Finally, at the end of my sixth-grade year and what seemed like an instant decision, our mom decided to leave Cecil and the farm. In a hurried frenzy, she moved my brother, herself, and me out of the farm country of Leonard, and back to Tulsa.

The short reunion between my birth father and my mom would end. I can honestly say that it was a relief not to have to see or listen to the dysfunctional banter between your mother and father, anymore.

Moving as many times as I did at a young age, and due to dysfunction in the family, it left me with a lot of uncertainty. Trusting others has always been a big issue for me. I can understand how my background created some emotional hindrances in my life, but it was also a blessing. It made me want something better for an occupation, something better financially, and more importantly, something better for my children.

Thankfully, right up over the hill that we seemed to be climbing in our early years, Tommy and I would have positive experiences waiting for us.

As the genius, Einstein put it, "In the middle of difficulty, lies opportunity."

4

WEST SIDE STORY

Somewhere, there's a place for us,
a time and place for us.
West Side Story…Broadway Play/Movie

The '50s and early '60s was a special time for those of us that grew up in that generation. Elvis Presley, Little Richard, Chuck Berry, Fat's Domino, and all the teen idols like Frankie Avalon and Annette Funicello, changed America.

Dick Clark's American Bandstand had all of us "swing dancing" to "rock & roll" after school, as we watched the Philadelphia show on our black and white televisions. The new music brought out teenage emotions and more independent behavior in most of us teenagers. Movies like "Rebel Without A Cause," which depicted adolescents rebelling against the norm, were starting to emerge. Though not true to life, Fonzie and Richie in the Happy Day's TV show and the movie American Graffiti portrayed many of the traits of teenagers that you would have seen on the Westside of Tulsa. It was an innocent time where behaviors such as smoking, drinking beer, or fist fighting, was regarded as bad behavior for young people. It was much different than this day and time of guns, knives, and the possibility of death, for any disagreement. As for me, I was trying to fit in and to not be any kind of troublemaker or rebel. I had my eyes set on doing the right things to better myself by associating with new friends, and doing well in school.

When my mom left Leonard and Cecil for good and moved us back to the Westside of Tulsa, it was a blessing. The Westside was a working-class community separated from the main parts of Tulsa by the Arkansas River.

Even though it was the right move for us to leave Leonard, Mom had very little money. Cecil did not offer or try to help my mom or us, in any way. We did not hear from him, nor did he make any attempt to keep us in his life.

To be able to move back to the Westside, Mom had to have help, financially, from her sister, Aunt Cora Blair. Aunt Cora helped rent us a house and bought some used furniture that we needed, very badly. We had taken some furniture from the farm, but because my parents had not kept up with monthly payments, the furniture company confiscated the furniture for delinquent payments. I remember all of us sleeping on the floor of the rent house on a blanket with no furniture for a few nights until Aunt Cora found us some used furniture. I thank our aunt Cora for bailing us out, and it wouldn't be the last time that she helped us.

Mom began looking for an extra job to add to her work as a waitress. Shortly, she would become employed at a glass manufacturing plant for the 3:00 p.m. to 11:00 p.m. night shift. Working as a waitress during the day and working on an assembly line at night, was very exhausting. With Mom working two jobs, and me at the age of thirteen, it was mostly up to me to be in charge of the house, as my brother and I took care of the chores.

The rent house we would occupy was in a section called old Red Fork. Many long-time Tulsans weren't even aware of the different areas of the Westside. Generally, only those who lived on that side of town knew the names of the small neighborhoods.

The area known as West Tulsa was just across the Arkansas River from downtown. Early in the morning when DX Sunray Oil & Gas was doing most of its work by refining gasoline, a very bad odor would emerge. Many Tulsans, who were living in finer areas of Tulsa, identified our neighborhoods with that unsavory smell. It wasn't pleasant, but I guess if you lived in West Tulsa, you got used to it. Another housing addition was Carbondale, where my Aunt Cora and Uncle Otto lived. It was a nice little neighborhood composed, mostly, of small working-class homeowners. Garden City was south of West Tulsa and further down the river. Many times, before the new Keystone Dam, there would be widespread flooding from the Arkansas River, in Garden City. Other small enclaves were Oakhurst and a small black neighborhood known as, South Haven.

School on the Westside was a catalyst for me. That's the place that helped give me a sense of community. While frequently moving, I may have been socially accepted in other schools, but the comfort I would come to know on the Westside was way beyond those that I'd previously attended.

I was enrolling, again, in a school where I was the new kid on the block. I knew only a few at Clinton Jr. High when I walked up to school, by myself. It was a scary and lonely feeling for me. However, I began to start sizing up my classmates immediately, and those I thought I might have a chance to get to know in class. I wanted to fit in, but I also wanted to make sure to choose and pursue the personalities that I thought I'd be more comfortable being around.

In attending Clinton for me, and Park elementary school for Tommy, it was an exciting time. Our schools were clean, they had good food, and we were able to socialize and make new friends. Being that money was tight for our mom, we looked forward to eating lunch at school because of the variety of food selections. For thirty-five cents, we'd be able to have a ready-made meal that we looked forward to, such as bean chowder or meatloaf, veggies, and a dessert. Sometimes it was hard for Mom to give us that amount of money for lunch, but even if there were free lunch programs, we were too proud to try to take advantage of it. It was as if it was a stigma for us to ask for any handout or free government help.

In addition to her jobs, Mom worked hard to make sure our clothes were clean, starched, and ironed, even though we usually had only two pairs of jeans during the school year. When our jeans developed holes in the knees, she'd patch them with store-bought iron-on patches. Torn jeans, in those days, were for those who couldn't afford jeans. It was not like today's torn fashion designer jeans. I guess because of my past; I still can't see sense in tearing jeans and making holes in them for a fashion look. But I guess that's just me? Times have changed.

The Clinton school environment was a little different because, for some reason, my gut had me feeling like I was going to be readily accepted in this school, and that I would love it. Many of the kids already knew each other and were former grade school or neighborhood friends. It took me a while, but I figured out that the athletes and the pretty girls were the ones I wanted to be around. The more I participated in school activities, the more teachers seem to start giving me some of the attention that I needed. Their encouragement gave me confidence and recognition, which began to ferment some private thoughts that I may be achieving a social life; with permanent and loyal friends I'd always wanted.

After Clinton Jr. High, I was on my way to Webster High School. It was known as a blue-collar high school with a tough reputation. But in my experience, much of that reputation was way overblown. The community was made up of hard-working middle and lower-middle-class families who demanded high standards of behavior for their children. Most of all, parents wanted their children to have a chance to succeed, and have a productive and better life than many of them had experienced.

By being involved in sports and different school activities with my classmates, and being accepted by my friends and their families, I began to feel more stable. The Westside neighborhood felt like home. I respect those Westside blue-collar values in which I grew up with, to this day. It truly was a place for us!

5

TEACHERS, MENTORS, AND DREAMS

"A mentor empowers a person to see
a possible future, and believe it can be obtained."
Shawn Hitchcock…Writer/Composer

There is a saying, "When the student is ready, the teacher will appear." Some attribute the quote to Buddha, the philosopher, but it makes no difference where it came from…it's true.

I felt my teachers at Webster high school were very dedicated and wanted "their kids" to have positive experiences. They all seemed to care about us as individuals while trying to push each of us toward our unique talents. I had my favorite teachers who helped me get through high school, not only academically and socially, but also athletically. Many educators didn't get enough recognition, such as Mrs. Crowe, a little English teacher who had her bluff on us jocks, or a Stagecraft/Speech teacher who tried his best to bring out our hidden creative talents. There were so many good teachers during my time in high school that it's difficult to mention them all, but they certainly influenced my student experience.

I did my best to participate and be a good student, but I enjoyed the available extra-curricular activities. I guess I can say that I thoroughly enjoyed going to school. In 2012, I had my fifty-year class reunion. A great many of my former classmates attended. As we talked, we all still remembered individual teachers, acquaintances, and funny stories that we shared about different personalities. Some of the characters that you would see in a movie, like "Grease," are spitting images of my old classmates and teachers.

As a young man, coaches would have a profound effect on me. While in junior high school from grades seven through nine, I had been a skinny kid. Many of my classmates matured earlier than me, so they were physically stronger when it came to football or most sports. I made up for my lack of strength by my willingness to keep competing, learning, and associating and with those who I thought would be successful. I wanted to play with the best and be included in that group. I tried extra hard to make the teams with the good athletes, whether I played much, or not.

I wasn't strong enough for football, and I didn't make the ninth-grade basketball team at Clinton. After I'd been cut from the basketball tryout, Coach Bill Allen of Webster asked the junior high coach to encourage me to come back on the team. Whatever it was that got them to ask me back, I do not know, but I was very happy that I had a second chance. That invitation to include me on the team had a positive influence on me, for the rest of my life. Little did I know, but Coach Bill Allen would not only become my basketball coach in high school, he would become my "lifelong mentor."

As a junior in high school, I was maturing, growing taller, and I was getting stronger. I'd grown from 6'1" as a sophomore to 6'6" by my senior year. At the end of my sophomore year at Webster, Coach Allen asked me to come to his office to visit. I didn't know what it was about, but I anxiously came to see him the next day. That visit elevated my self-image and gave me an uplifting feeling that I'll always remember. On a chalkboard, he'd written the names of all of our current basketball players. As he pointed to the list, he then asked me, "Where do you think you rank on this list of players, from top to bottom?" As I studied the board, I sheepishly told him that I thought I was somewhere in the middle. He then pointed at the list and said,

"As far as potential, here's where I think you should be in relation to each of the other players on our team." To be honest, I didn't know what the word "potential" meant? He then pointed at the board and let me know that he thought that I was second only to Richard Calmus, who was one of the two best athletes in school. Then, as he looked at me straight in the eye, he said, "If you work hard and keep doing what you've been doing, I think you can get a college scholarship!"

Wow! I'd never thought about a college scholarship in my life. Like the quote stated at the start of this chapter, "When the student is ready, the teacher will appear!" Someone had just given me a new vision and goal to work toward, which was a college scholarship. Up until that time, I was reacting and striving to do the best I could, every day. Now there was something planted in the back of my mind. "College!"

Fortunately for me, our team was the top-ranked team in the State of Oklahoma in 1962. We were having a great year, and a great deal of attention was given to us, in the Oklahoma City and Tulsa sports sections, of the newspapers. Calmus was the best player on our team and was to become a high school All-American. Nationwide, coaches knew about him. Recruiting wasn't like it is today, in which coaches have film of a player sent to them to decipher whether you were a good fit with their team and system. Back then, a coach had to watch a potential recruit work out and play in real games, to evaluate if they were good enough to play for their team. There were not any basketball camps or AAU tournaments, as there is today, where a player could be observed and evaluated. While in high school on the Westside, most of us were expected to play summer baseball or work in the summer, and take up sports again when school started. As for me, in high school, summer was a time that I worked to help my mom pay for groceries and rent.

In my senior year and during one of our late-season games at Webster, an assistant basketball coach from the University of Oklahoma came to watch our team play. In addition to coaches wanting to follow our team and watch us play, the other team had a 6'9" player that colleges were very interested in seeing, as well. As luck would have it, I had a great game against the opposing player and his team, that night. After the game, the assistant coach from OU congratulated us on the win and let Richard and me know that he'd be back in touch with us, very soon. The next week, not only did OU offer Calmus a four-year scholarship to play basketball at the University of Oklahoma, they also offered me a four-year scholarship. I was stunned and, almost, overwhelmed.

After the basketball season was over, Calmus, Carl Morton (football/baseball player), and I went on a recruiting visit to OU, where we met the famous Football Coach and Athletic Director, Bud Wilkinson. Bud was like a god in Oklahoma. He was the one who made OU famous with forty-seven straight victories in football. Many loyal OU fans thought that Bud put Oklahoma on the map. For us to be in his office and personally talk to him, we were almost in a trance. He welcomed us and asked us to please consider their offer of an OU scholarship, and that he'd love to have us be a "Sooner!" I was sold before I even stepped foot on campus.

Here it was, right in front of me. A paid college education from, not only a major university, but also it was The University of Oklahoma! Four years, all expenses paid, which included room, board (meals), tuition, and $15.00 monthly, for laundry. Until Coach Bill Allen gave me a vision, I had not known what I was going to do after high school. The only thing that I'd known was manual work and carrying a lunch bucket. Other students had some discussion of college, but not everyone in our neighborhood was planning on a higher degree of education. Having been offered that OU basketball scholarship sent me on to a new journey, which had been totally unexpected.

One of my personal basketball experiences with my mentor, Coach Allen, still sticks in my mind. It was my junior year in high school, and our team was leading Will Rogers high school by one point, with little time left on the clock. After a game timeout, Rogers would have the ball when it was to be put into play, again. Coach told our team to "play position, don't foul, and make them make a basket to beat us." As time was running out, Rogers put the ball in play, and my man went up to shoot. I extended my arm and hand to act like I was going to block his shot. As a foul was called on me, my heart sank. If they made the free throws, they win. I wasn't supposed to foul. The player proceeded to make two free throws, and we lost the game. It was heartbreaking for me, as I had let the seniors down and, most of all, Coach Allen down. I was devastated.

After the game, Coach immediately had a meeting with our team. He said, "I just want everyone to know, as I saw it, that was the cleanest blocked shot that I can ever remember." He followed with, "but we can't dwell on that referee's call. Alan did the right thing to help us win. It just didn't work in our favor, this time." Coach took all of the pressure off of me. In reality, I don't think he knew if I had touched the ball or fouled the Rogers player by touching his hand, slightly, or not. The call could have gone either way. To this day, I don't know if I touched that player's hand, but that's not important. Coach had my back, and I loved him for believing in me, in front of my teammates.

Coach Allen passed away in 2014. In preparing for his service, his minister asked me to come to his office for a comment regarding my relationship with Coach, as my mentor. When asked, I replied to the minister, "Coach gave me a dream and pointed me toward a future path. He always made it clear that it was up to me to work hard and take advantage of the opportunities that would come my way!"

At Webster high school, I developed as a young man, as an athlete, and as a student. That special time set the tone for the rest of my life. I'm deeply indebted to Coach Bill Allen, teachers, and the long-lasting friendships that I developed. I have always cherished those challenging and fun times in my life.

I feel so fortunate!

6

WORK & RESPONSIBILITY

"Responsibility is the price of Freedom."
Elbert Hubbard...Author

I had just turned seventeen in the summer of 1962. Before going off to college at OU, I was employed again at Flint Steel Corporation, the same as the summer before my senior year in high school. In future summers, I would also work at Flint, but it would be in different work areas throughout my time in college. Even though I had a scholarship, I had to work because I needed to be responsible for any clothes or unknown expenses during the school year.

I had the 3:00 p.m. to 11:00 p.m. shift at Flint that first summer, in which I made $1.40 an hour. The wage was great for someone my age. Because Flint Steel was a company that had a labor union, I had to pay thirty dollars in union dues to join, before I could report for work. While working eight to ten hours a day, my paycheck was about forty dollars a week, after taxes. I split some of the proceeds of my check to help my mom, with some of our bills.

As a welder's helper, my job was known by everyone as a "grinder." That sounds weird when I say it now, but then it seemed like a dream job. Flint made steel oil derricks used for drilling by companies searching for new oil. When assembling the derricks, different beams of steel were welded together by a welder to form the drilling rig. The welds on the various parts that made up the platform had to be smoothed and polished by a handheld spinning disk. Soot and sparks would fly everywhere. After an eight or ten-hour workday, black soot covered me from head to toe. I was filthy, but by having a job, I felt successful because I was making some hard-earned money.

It felt good to have a job and work. Working hard work had been ingrained in me, and most of my friends, at an early age. Those expectations were passed on to most of us by the mom and dads of the previous generation.

I learned a lot about life while working in a manufacturing plant. I think the most important experience was visiting with guys who had been working in a factory for fifteen to twenty years. They'd work at hard labor, while eagerly waiting for the whistle to blow for rest and lunch breaks. We'd hurriedly fast walk to the break areas for lunch, just as if it was like at a grade school recess, where youngsters ran to the playground.

Being a young man and also very energetic, the long-time union employees would let me know when I seemed to be too eager and working to fast. By finishing my work assignment too quickly, my fellow cohorts would say to me, "Don't work your way out of a job, boy!" Which meant, if we get a task finished too soon and there are not many projects in the immediate pipeline, the company could lay you off till they had more work activity in the system. As well, when you were laid off, it didn't necessarily mean that they would hire you back when business picked up. With the uncertainty of long-term employment, many of my fellow work buddies always gave me the same input, which was to go to college and don't make this your full-time occupation. My first employment in a manufacturing facility, plus guidance from older employees, solidified my desire to look into other areas for a future profession. I did not want to be carrying a lunch bucket every day while trying to support a family, as did many of them. As much as I loved the feeling of having a job, I knew that working at hard labor was not what I wanted to do for the rest of my life.

I do recall one funny story when the plant manager came out of his office to walk through the plant. Along with another manager, they were meandering through the facility to check things out. They both wore a white shirt with a tie, and the plant manager was puffing on a pipe protruding from his mouth. Of course, all the factory workers were cussing the manager behind his back and saying how "uppity" he was, and how he looked like an asshole, among other things. Being a team-oriented type guy, I joined in on the criticism behind the manager's back, because it seemed like the thing to do.

Later in my life, as a young salesman, I called on Flint Steel to try to generate some new business for our company. It brought back some fun memories knowing it was the same place I'd worked in the summers, throughout college. After arranging a sales meeting and proceeding to try to convince the new plant manager to purchase our products, he said to me, "Come on with me, let me show you our facility!" I immediately had a flashback of my summer work experience in my college days! I felt nervous because I would be walking into the plant dressed in a coat and tie and, all the while, knowing what the workers were going to say among themselves about "me." The shoe was now on the other foot. I laughed on the inside, knowing of off-colored words being shared between them, as I sashayed with the "boss" in front of them. I tried to look and make eye contact with various workers, as I smiled and mentally communicated my approval of their silent bitching. It's crazy how life changes. I guess the old saying, "what goes around, comes around" is true. However, I can honestly say, I was glad and very pleased I was on the other side of the work spectrum, this time around.

While the money I made working in the summers helped, I was ready to move on to college. At OU, scholarship athletes received a check for fifteen dollars a month, which they called laundry money, along with my athletic scholarship. Being on scholarship, athletes could not work during the school year, and fifteen dollars was like a gift to me. The small amount went much further back then, and with my room and board paid, that's all I had during the school year.

My mom had remarried when I'd been in high school. Even though I was away from home and in college, a family problem would periodically arise. There were times that my mother would get in touch with me, and I'd travel home and have to get into the middle of her and her husband's difficulties. One example is when my college coach, Bob Stevens, informed me before one of our practices that he'd gotten a call from a relative of mine. He said that my mom had been arrested and that I needed to come home. To this day, I'm not sure who made the call, but I was embarrassed because I didn't want anyone to know about my family problems. I was fearful and scared at the same time because I didn't know all of the information, or what had happened. Coach Stevens said for me to go home and do whatever I needed to do and not worry about practice. Because I didn't have a car or money, I hitchhiked from Norman to Tulsa to see what was going on? I had no idea how to help, at the time, but I knew that I needed to try to help fix the situation, if possible?

After I arrived home, I found that my aunt Cora had gotten my mom arrested and committed to the Tulsa County jail. By saying a relative was mentally unstable, a family member could use a legal procedure toward a relative, in which the defendant would have to prove his or her mental competency. Aunt Cora had wanted my grandma Barnes, who had been staying with Mom, to move in with her. She filed a motion with the City of Tulsa stating that my mom's mental state was a danger to my feeble grandmother's welfare. By being arrested on a Friday, that meant Mom was going to spend the weekend in jail because no one in city hall would rule on her case over the weekend.

I knew only one person that was either an attorney or had anything to do with the law. His name was Clinton Riggs, the Chief of Police in Tulsa. I had briefly dated his daughter, Michelle, in high school, and was still friends with her at OU. It was tough for me because it was unusual for an inexperienced Westsider to ask for personal help from the Chief of Police of Tulsa. Because of my friendship with his daughter and because he was a caring and exceptional man, he helped me acquire an attorney.

On Saturday, which was the next day, Mr. Riggs, the attorney, and myself met with a judge that Mr. Riggs had called upon to help me. I was embarrassed, uneasy, and scared, but at the same time, I was very thankful to have someone so high up in law enforcement on my side. I will always feel grateful for the help of Mr. Riggs.

When we went in front of a judge, Mr. Riggs and the attorney did most of the talking, but I had to be the one to tell the judge the story of how I felt that my Aunt Cora shouldn't have had Mom arrested. I let the judge know that it was a personal grudge between two sisters.

Because of Mr. Riggs's help, Mom was released and went home with her husband, Leroy, and his three kids. Mom never acknowledged my help and never really thanked me for coming home from college and getting involved. She would only laugh about how ridiculous it was for Aunt Cora to have her jailed, and vowed to get back at her. She used various derogatory statements and curse words to express those feelings. I just wanted to get it behind me and get back to OU and practice. I needed to get back to something normal.

Even though Mom was married to her third husband, he was not involved in standing up for her or attempt and try to rectify the crazy situation. Maybe it was a lack of knowledge or insecurity on his part, but as an adult, he seemed to have no clue, nor even made an effort. He wasn't involved at all in getting her out of jail. As a young man in college, the responsibility had been all on me.

My mom never forgave her sister for having gone to authorities and have her arrested, even though my aunt had helped us with much needed financial help, in the past.

When I was at OU, or even in my early years of marriage, I never knew when those types of family problems were going to arise. After Mom got out of jail, I hitchhiked back to Norman to try to get back to my classes and to practice on Monday. I wanted out of Tulsa and away from my mother and her husband.

Looking back at that situation over fifty-plus years ago, I now feel I had passed a test that weekend. I started to become an adult because I had to solve a very stressful situation. I had been the one that had to take on family difficulties that, probably, should have been handled by older adults.

One valuable lesson I learned was not to be afraid to reach out to the right people and ask for their help. I've found that your circle of acquaintances and friends are very important in life, and to not take them lightly.

When I made it back to Norman, I can honestly say that I felt that I was home. I was comfortable with my teammates and coaches, and that environment gave me a sense of stability. At that particular time in my life, I came to the realization that my home was now,

The University of Oklahoma!

7

BOOMER SOONER

"I Have Never Let My Schooling Interfere With My Education."
Mark Twain…Author/Humorist

My first year in college at OU was just like most students, and that was getting to know new people and trying to make it in a different environment. I was not prepared for college, as I'd just left a small high school, and was now at a major university with fifteen to twenty thousand students.

There weren't any computers, email, cell phones, or technological advances to make it easy to enroll, in those days. To enroll, I stood in long lines at the basketball Fieldhouse, while not knowing what the hell I was doing. We were told that during the season, we had to be dressed and on the court at three o'clock. Knowing that we could not have any classes after one o'clock, it was hectic trying to find basic freshman classes that only fit morning time slots. Because of having to take those morning classes, I ended up taking a couple of challenging courses that would, eventually, kick my ass that first semester.

As far as where I'd be living in Norman, the OU football and basketball player's athletic dorm was in Washington House. It was east and directly across the street from the south end zone of the football stadium. OU was known nationally for football and I'd always been a huge fan, so for me, it was an honor to be housed across the street in a prime location, while attending an OU football game. I felt important on those days when I'd walk across the street to a game, while others traveled long distances for that experience.

The football players had the first three floors of "Wash House." Basketball players were on the fourth floor, which was the highest in the building. Many times, after a grueling basketball practice, those four flights felt like we were climbing a mountain. Our dorm was the newer dorm for the jocks, and very clean. We all ate in the athletic dining hall where the food was plentiful and, consistently, better than I ever could have imagined. I remember that it was the first time I'd ever tasted a real steak. I'd had a hamburger steak or chicken fried steak, but never a choice cut of beef. The OU athletic training table fed us well. I was a skinny 170 lbs. when I started school, but when I left OU after my senior year, I weighed in at 215 lbs. Like I said, the food was great.

The first day that I arrived, I met my new roommate, Joe Bogan. He was a 6′ 7″ center from El Reno, Oklahoma. Joe was book smart, and academics seemed to be a little easier for him than this city boy. I lacked in study habits in college, even though I had above-average grades in high school. Later on, because of Joe being an example, watching him gave me a glimpse of how I needed to study and what I needed to do to survive, academically. Joe has been a lifelong college friend, and I was fortunate he was the person that I was paired up with when I was entering a new part of my life. Joe became a federal prison warden just like his father had been at the El Reno Federal Prison. He later moved up into the ladder of leadership in the Federal Bureau of Prisons.

Even though I'm jumping ahead, I have to tell this one story about Joe's dad and the federal prison. At the end of our senior year and after our basketball eligibility at OU, Joe's dad asked a group of us to play the El Reno Federal Prison, inmate team. A group of our basketball graduates agreed. We all said, why not?

We didn't know what to expect, but I'll never forget the experience. As we entered the prison, we were strip-searched in a holding area before entering the prison yard. When we did proceed to walk out into an open area of the prison to enter into the gym, we were met with frequent catcalls, whistles, and verbal sexual innuendos, which made us feel a little uncomfortable. We just smiled, but we were really out of our element with the prisoners staring down at us from balconies, outside their cells. We were sure happy to move into a holding area by the gymnasium.

When we entered the empty gym, we immediately started to warm up after taking off our warm-up jerseys and sweat pants. In those days, our basketball shorts were just as the name calls for; they were "short" and almost up to our ass. All of a sudden, we hear very loud basketball type whistles as two large doors at the end of the gym began to open. In a single file, the prisoners walked into the facility and were immediately seated in the bleachers, on both sides of the court. The wooden bleachers were ones like you'd find at old high school, which were folded out and down close to the floor. When the game began, and we were matched up against their starting five, it seemed that every time we lined up for a free throw and bent over looking for a rebound, there was usually some laughing and sexual comments toward us, from the bleachers. As each of us players looked at each other throughout the game, we had an uneasy look in our eyes. I'm sure they could see the insecurity in my eyes! As I recall, we didn't play hard and just wanted to get the game over with and get the hell out of there. Of course, we lost the game because of not being focused, but that didn't matter because we were damn glad it was over. However, it was a memory that I'd be able to share with my grandkids fifty years later.

As Joe and I started to get settled in as roommates, it became apparent that all the players were trying to see where we all would fit in socially. As jocks that lived together in the athletic dorm, we were trying to promote ourselves to each other by acting confident and trying to be cautiously social. With that, the jock dialogue began to escalate. By jock dialogue, I refer to the teasing and crude pranks among the athletes. There was always talk about girls, roughhousing, grab ass, and having regular "boy talk!" We all were athletes and had that macho mentality that we thought was necessary to fulfill our egos while living together in close quarters. Some of our stories and lies were tossed back and forth very freely and were off-color many times. Many of the fraternities and sororities labeled the athletes at Washington House, as "Jock Animals." But truthfully, let's blame the jock reputation and everything inappropriate on the football players. They out-numbered us, so that is the only fair thing to do!

At OU in 1962, freshmen players were not eligible to play on the varsity. The NCAA felt that those right out of high school were not mature enough mentally or physically to pass classes, and play ball against older players. I do know that it was good for me not having to compete against more mature players to make the varsity team. However, we did have a freshman team and separate practices, as well as playing eight scheduled freshman games. Our freshman rival was Oklahoma A&M, which later became Oklahoma State University. That game was our freshman basketball motivation, and the game was always directly in our sites from the start of practice. To this day, I still tease my Oklahoma State friends by calling them "Aggies" in reference to the school's past as an Agricultural and Mechanical school. It pisses them off, but I loved to "turn the knife" in them, anytime I get the chance.

I did well as a freshman in basketball, but not so good in school. My study habits, playing basketball, and scheduling some difficult classes had affected me, academically. At the end of the school year, I thought of quitting at OU and attending a smaller school because of my grades. I'd had a "B" in algebra and trigonometry in high school, but the professor of college algebra kicked my ass with an "F." I guess my Webster education in math was a little anemic. I'd also say that I, probably, bullshitted my way through Mr. Holt's algebra class in high school!

After the first semester and Christmas break, I traveled back to Tulsa and went by my old high school to visit with Coach Allen. I was nervous about the visit, as I began to tell Coach of my thoughts of leaving OU and taking a scholarship at Northeastern State College. As only Coach Allen could do, he grimaced when he wanted you to know that he probably didn't agree with what you'd just said, or there were doubts about the subject discussed. He then proceeded to give me some valuable advice that would have a positive effect on me in the future.

He said, "Whether it's right or wrong, your degree from OU will carry more weight in the job market, later in life. I'm not going to tell you what to do, but I know you can be successful if you persevere and use your potential." There it was, again. It was the one word he used to motivate me that day in his office. Potential!

After that meeting, and doing some self-analysis, I realized that I'd already progressed further in education than I'd ever imagined. I thought to myself, I did have potential, so why not reach higher. After much thought, I decided that failure was not an option and realized that I hadn't applied myself. I had not done what it took to succeed, and that was to focus on putting in the hard work, time, and energy toward my classes. I had let my thoughts wander into a "woe is me" mentality. Without knowing it, I had regressed into thinking that maybe I'm not smart enough or that I was not worthy of an OU education. Overcoming those self-deprecating feelings was a valuable lesson that paid off for me, many times over. With that said, I bucked up. It just took someone to jar me back to the reality that I could do whatever I wanted if I focused my energy on academics. I went back to OU for the second semester and finished my freshman year with a new attitude, and better than average grades.

After working at Flint Steel again that summer, in the fall of 1963, I went back to OU and decided on a major. When I had gone off to college as a freshman, I had no idea what I was going to do in life or even had an inkling of a major. My first academic counselor at OU just threw me into any class to get me out of his office. He didn't seem to care. But to be fair, I also didn't know what to ask him about academics or have any idea of what I wanted to pursue, as a career.

At the beginning of the school year at OU, I was talking to one of my teammates when I noticed that he was looking at some school material. Curiously, I asked about it? He said to me, "These are all the classes I have to take to graduate, as an education major." In looking at his written plan that his guidance counselor had given to him, I realized that I had been attending college, but I had no plan or even had an idea of what it would take to get to the "end game!" That end game was graduation!

While in that discussion with my teammate, it hit me! I could do what he's doing! Another light went off in my head, as I came to realize that I could be a teacher and coach, just like Coach Allen. I guess you could say that it was a "Eureka" moment for me! By having a copy of that curriculum, I would not just be taking the basic college classes. I would now take courses needed to become a teacher by pursuing a path toward a Bachelor of Science Degree in Education. I was excited, as a sense of relief came over me. I was starting to figure out the college life of academics and not just basketball.

My years at OU were a transition for me. By meeting new acquaintances and teammates from different geographic areas, I not only was receiving an academic education but also a much broader view of the way others lived in their communities. I went on to graduate in 1966 with credentials to become a Certified Teacher in the State of Oklahoma.

As a senior, OU coach Bob Stevens handed out team awards. That year, I was voted by my teammates to receive the Leadership Award, as well as the Humorist Award. Those times were special. I had changed from a lanky, insecure, and skinny high school kid, to a college graduate, who'd played on a major college basketball team.

I've always felt fortunate to have the OU experience. Some of my dearest friends are from those important years. I loved my teammates!

As the old OU fight song says:

Boomer Sooner, Boomer Sooner

I'm a Sooner born, and Sooner bred

And when I die, I'll be Sooner dead.

8

MR. AXLEY

"Being a new teacher is like trying
to fly an airplane, while building it."
Rick Smith...Teacher

"Choose a job you love, and you'll never have to work a day in your life!" That famous piece of wisdom is from the great Chinese philosopher, Confucius. It sounds good, but I've found very few individuals that knew of a job they loved, very early in life. As adults, they first had to work and find a way to pay for the things that they needed. After food, clothing, and shelter, what comes next are the choices you make to enhance your status by working to survive the everyday challenges of society. I was no different.

I didn't have a vision of becoming an engineer, doctor, lawyer or have one of those professional jobs, but I could identify with coaching and teaching because I'd been around it throughout my school days. I was familiar with the occupation, and it seemed to make sense for me. Was I planning early in my childhood to become a teacher, coach, or salesman, while working my way through life? Did I have goals for my professional path? The answers are a definite, No! As a young man, I was not even thinking about what I'd do in the future.

I'd had a childhood dream of a house on a hill with modern conveniences, but no thought of a path toward that dream.

In 1966, I graduated from the University of Oklahoma, and it was now time to move out into the real world. In August of that year, I applied and was scheduled to interview for a teaching and coaching position at Star Spencer high school. Initially, Star Spencer had been the eight through twelfth-grade school for the little town of Spencer, Oklahoma. As Oklahoma City was growing in landmass, Spencer, and it's public school, was annexed by the City in the mid-1960s.

I was nervous in my formal interview with the Oklahoma City personnel director, but after also being interviewed by the Star Spencer high school principal, I ended up being accepted to teach history, physical education, and become an assistant coach for basketball. I was excited that I now had a full-time professional teaching job.

A great deal of me attaining that first teaching assignment was by having graduated and playing basketball at the University of Oklahoma. Many young basketball graduates wanted and pursued coaching jobs in the late '60s. As Coach Allen had previously related to me, a degree from OU would be very beneficial if I was to compete for a teaching and basketball coaching position. The truth is, it was!

As a young teacher, I soon found how difficult it was to be in charge of high school students. Because I was only two or three years older than the seniors that I'd be teaching in high school, I felt that I had to always act much older. It was weird hearing someone call me Mr. Axley or coach Axley. Being just out of college, I was used to most of my teammates just calling me "Ax." When I heard my new students give reference to Mr. Axley for the first time, I thought to myself, "I guess I'm now qualified as a professional adult?" I vividly recall wondering if I was ready to be in charge of a high school classroom? I was questioning myself, and having doubts about teaching and disciplining high school students, who were close to my age of twenty-two.

In the fall of 1966, the small schools of Dungee and Arcadia were annexed into Oklahoma City. The all-black students in those schools would be attending school at Star Spencer, which was made up of, mostly, blue-collar white residents. The new racial integration process made it difficult for a new teacher, like myself. Not only was I not familiar with how to teach, we were also in the middle of integrating a public school! I'd played ball with blacks, and they were my teammates, but when it came to trying to walk a fine line of how to talk or teach an integrated group of high school students, I was not sure of myself.

As well as having some insecurity of teaching students, I also had responsibilities as the assistant basketball coach. An added part of that position had to do with the extra assignment of having to get a chauffeur's license. As a basketball assistant, I was the one that was to drive the athletic bus for our basketball players to attend away games, or any team activity away from the school. My salary was $5,250.00 a year, plus a bonus of $500 a year for coaching. Teachers' pay wasn't much by today's standards. However, it was a job.

Later on, I'd get another $300 per year for the important job of taking care of the candy machine. Of course, I say that in jest, I guess? Making sure the vending machine was full of treats, while also emptying the coin collection tray, was of high priority for my principal. I'm sure I needed the $300 because I stepped up and took the added assignment when he first offered it to me. My buddies kidded me, as they said, "Can't believe that he's trusting you with the money collected from the candy machine?" Even though I was out of college, my buddies never missed a chance to "razz" me.

I learned a great deal from other teachers and, especially, the coaches in the athletic department. For that first year, it was trial and error for me most of the time. I recall getting an ulcer, or what I thought was an ulcer, due to the everyday stress of wanting to succeed in my new challenge. I was trying very hard to find my way in a new environment while adjusting from being a student right out of college. It was challenging and sometimes uncomfortable for me.

Some of the teachers and coaches were very interesting individuals, and I could not have had better colleagues, to help me through my first year. But another particular individual was unique and was someone that I truly respected.

June Dawkins was the Star Spencer principal. Even though the name "June" was regarded as a female name, Mr. Dawkins was definitely not a female. June was a "man's, man." His persona always reminds me of the old song by Johnny Cash titled, "A Boy Named Sue." Being a male with a female name made him a hard ass. At about the age of fifty, Mr. Dawkins was a tough "hombre." He took no shit and didn't expect you to take any off of the students. In his school, you were not just a teacher; you were also a disciplinarian. His mantra was, "If you don't have rules and discipline, you can't teach." Period! I'd seen him run across a field and successfully tackle young male students, as they were trying to skip school. They had messed with the wrong guy when they broke the rules. I had much respect for June Dawkins.

The athletic director and football coach was Carl Twidwell. He was thirty-eight years old and, to most of us younger coaches, he was considered the "old man" of the group. But, that was not the case. Even though he was bald and had a wrinkled brow, there was always a smile on his face. As friendly as he was, we all knew that he could kick most people's butt, including any of us young coaches. In recalling one incident when my fellow coaches and I attended a high school all-star baseball game, we'd parked too close to a car in the parking lot. The location on the lot seemed to make it difficult for another driver to back out of their parking space. I don't know whether they were students or not, but three young men confronted us and, after surveying the three of us, said to Twid, "Old man, move this car or we'll kick your ass!" We knew the young guy made a mistake by picking the wrong one of us to challenge. It was over in a minute or two. Twid got the mouthy one down and chewed his ear halfway off, while the two others ran. He wasn't even winded and was grinning like he'd just had a bite of apple pie. It was a sight to see! This incident re-affirmed to me that you didn't want to ever make Twid angry with you.

John Tatum was about four years older than me. He had been a football linebacker at OU and had also been a graduate assistant under the famous coach, Bud Wilkinson. He was now an assistant football and head baseball coach at Star. We quickly became friends because of our OU background. John was a straight shooter and straight to the point when in a discussion, and it's safe to say that he was not shy. Later on, John would be a helpful contact in the business world for me. Twid, Tatum, and David Self, the wrestling coach, were all from Heavener, a small town in southeastern Oklahoma. They all were very likable and very tough competitors. I had a lot of respect for their small-town values and their work ethic. I feel blessed that I had them as colleagues and mentors for my first professional coaching position. I was the youngest of the group and honored that they accepted me as one of them.

In the classroom, students tried to test me right away. I wanted to be their teacher/coach and gain respect and discipline, but I found that it was not easy to do. In one American History class, coach Selph and I had to teach 120 students in the auditorium. While one of us lectured and taught the lesson of the day, the other would walk around to keep discipline. Yes, we paddled or gave swats to those that seemed not to want to follow directions. Corporal punishment was legal in public schools, at the time, so that you could use a paddle for discipline. We'd be arrested today for disciplining students the way we did back then, but it was an acceptable form of punishment. I wasn't comfortable giving "swats" to those that were not much younger than me when they acted up, but it was part of the culture, and it was expected of us, teachers.

One of my teaching assignments was a physical education class with about fifty students. One day when I was the only coach in the gym, I challenged a student to follow some basic rules. All of a sudden, rather than abide by those rules, he decided he was ready to fight and, unexpectedly, took a swing at me. In trying to curtail the student's wild punches, I took him hard to the ground and planted a knee on his back, to stabilize him. While holding him down, I looked up from our small skirmish to see that the remaining students in the gym had surrounded us. The young men had done what many students would do anytime there was a fight or altercation, and that was to get a better view of those taking part in the action and sometimes participate.

I remember feeling fearful that a small group of the remaining troublemakers in the class might jump on me because I had no adult help in the gym. I was alone. Thankfully, one of the students ran into the office and alerted another teacher to come help with the situation. The unruly senior student was a white kid who was thrown out of school immediately by the principal, June Dawkins. The student did not graduate that year and had to go to summer school due to that incident. I felt sad for the student, but June Dawkins had his rules. As I said, he was a tough "hombre!"

The teaching profession was not what I'd envisioned, while at Star Spencer. My high school days at Webster high school seemed to have been more civil and respectful.

I was thankful that I'd had help from some of my fellow teachers and coaches at Star, but even with their support, I feel that I meandered my way through several difficult situations. I did have a lot of uncertainty in whether I liked being a teacher? I questioned if I was in the right place, or the right occupation? Those questions kept lingering after that first year.

As the year ended, I took a deep breath and said to myself, "You did it!"

But, Mr. Axley, do you want to do it, again?

9

THE MILITARY

"The aim of military training is not just to
prepare for battle, but to make them long for it."
Lewis Simpson…Author

The Vietnam War was a catalyst for turmoil in the mid-1960's, and early '70s. The conflict made it a priority to target young men to be called to serve their country through a draft lottery system. It was the luck of the draw, whether it would be your name being drawn for military service, or whether your status would be postponed, until a later date.

If you were a college student, a married man, or had a particular skill needed at home in the U.S., your draft status could be deferred. Which meant, it would delay your eligibility for the draft until the government had a desire for more soldiers, and changed the qualifications.

I'd had a draft deferment for being married, but now that the war was raging in Vietnam, they needed more men. In the winter of 1967 and during my second year of teaching, I was drafted to serve in the U.S. Army. When I informed my high school principal about my new draft status, he let me know that he'd like for me to stay and teach. Mr. Dawkins asked me if I would entertain serving in the Oklahoma

Army National Guard? Instead of Army active duty, I'd be stationed in Oklahoma City, until I was called into active duty. When I agreed to pursue his offer, he then arranged a meeting with the OKC public school's personnel director. After my interview, the director contacted an Army Colonel in the Oklahoma National Guard and asked him if there were any openings in his OKC unit. I interviewed for an opening and was accepted.

After all the paperwork, I enlisted for a six-year period of service, which would be from 1967 to 1973.

Everyone drafted or in the Army National Guard went to Basic Training and Advanced Infantry Training with Regular Army recruits. In early January of 1968, I left Oklahoma City Will Rogers Airport and traveled to El Paso, Texas, which was near the Ft. Bliss Army Training Center. The city of El Paso was just across the border from Juarez, Mexico. Along with other guardsmen and drafted Army recruits from Oklahoma, we were now on our way for those eight weeks of Basic Training, and another eight weeks of Advanced Infantry Training.

After the initial entry into the life of a new cadet, everything was planned for you from 4:00 a.m. till you went to bed at 8:00 p.m., or later. The beginning basics of Army training were of getting up early, making your bed, taking orders, training physically, and being responsible for, not only yourself but for your fellow soldiers. Drill Sergeants were constantly moving everyone around to different locations while screaming and yelling with intense intimidation.

I was twenty-three years old with a college education, I'd had a professional teaching position, and I was in top physical shape. Many of the Army draftees were eighteen-year-old kids who had no idea about Army life. Early on, the Drill Sergeant pulled me aside and told me that I was to become a platoon leader for my fellow recruits. Having my room was a big deal, as I did not have to sleep and take care of my responsibilities, while listening to gripes, farts, and bitching, from fellow soldiers in their living quarters. I felt lucky. Later on, another platoon leader would join me to form a leadership team.

KEEP ON, KEEPIN' ON!

After that first eight weeks of Basic Training, we had been indoctrinated with the Army disciplines of taking orders, marching in formation, weapons training, physical competition, and overnight combat maneuvers. Having done very well in the Army combat tasks, physical challenges, and written tests, two Lieutenants encouraged me to attend OCS/Officers Candidate School with the Regular Army. The Army was in need of leaders and officers. As a competitor, and having been given an accolade as the top trainee in my Army battalion, it made me feel good about myself. However, after OCS training, it definitely would be meant for me to be sent straight to Vietnam, as a second Lieutenant. Being a competitive athlete and getting caught up in the Army mentality, I actually thought about it. I guess it was because you are so hyped up and brainwashed in the ways of the military, and duty to the country, that you tend to want to be part of it.

The next day a Sergeant, who'd served in Vietnam, pulled me aside when he heard of the officers visiting with me. Sergeant Rice asked me, "Corporal Axley, regarding your discussions yesterday, of becoming an officer, I want you to know something. When you are the lead Lieutenant walking across a rice paddy in Vietnam looking for the enemy, who do you think their sniper is going to shoot first?" Thinking he was trying to trick me into giving him a stupid answer, which was the usual protocol in the Army training camp, I said, "I don't know, Sergeant?" Sgt. Rice was about 5'11" in height, so as he looked up at me and then proceeded to point a gun-like finger at my temple, he said, "It would be the tallest soldier, Corporal Axley. So, being as tall as you are, I'd think about your decision, very seriously." With that said, I took a step back and realized I need to pay more attention to the severity of my decision, and not just feel good about those officers blowing smoke up my ass.

There was also another primary reason I decided not to pursue the offer of OCS.

Jim Cumiskey, the older brother of my wife, Carol, had been an Air Force pilot. Eight months earlier, in the summer of 1967, his plane had been shot down, and he was killed in Vietnam. Jim's funeral was a very sad event. His death and the grief I saw with the family played a major role in me not taking any Officer Candidate School Training. I couldn't imagine Carol and her family having to worry about another person that went off to war. At the time, we didn't give enough respect for the ones who have risked their lives in our wars. We don't give enough respect and attention for parents like my former in-laws, Paul and Betty Cumiskey, who lose their sons or daughters in foreign wars. The parents and families of fallen soldiers are the forgotten ones.

Even though I spent six years in the Army National Guard, I did feel guilty that I didn't go to "Nam" for many years. I thought it was almost unpatriotic not to serve your country on active duty. But it was the right thing to do. At lunch recently, I confessed my guilt to John Admire, a former high school basketball teammate, who is a retired General in the Marine Corp. He served three tours in Vietnam after he graduated from OU. When I gave John my thoughts regarding my feelings of serving National Guard duty vs. the regular Army, he said to me, "Never feel guilty, Alan. We're all Americans, and we all serve differently, but we all serve." John explained that he'd been like many young men who could see the danger in going to Vietnam. He said that he told his dad that he was thinking of trying to avoid the draft. John said that his dad, a Navy veteran of World War II, frowned at him until John quickly explained that he was joining the "Marines." John's dad smiled and said to him, "That's an unusual way to dodge the draft!"

With that, John said he found his niche in the Marines and served proudly until he recently retired.

Today, as I see Americans vacationing and having a good time in Vietnam, and the U.S. recognizing the country as a preferred trading partner, I think to myself… What was it all about?

We now honor the names of 58,220 American Soldiers killed in action on the Vietnam Memorial Wall in Washington D.C.

10

HOME IS WHERE THE HEART IS!

Who Says You Can't Go Home!
Bon Jovi...Singer/Song

After my sixteen weeks of training, it was good to get back home that spring of 1968. I would go back to work at Star Spencer in the fall, and I was very pleased that they'd held my teaching and coaching position for me.

A few months later, we added Steve, our first son, to the family on September 29, 1968. It was a big change in our life trying to learn how to take care of a baby. It was very different for us, but fun. One of my favorite memories is of the first time that we went out to eat, after bringing Steve home from the hospital. We pulled out of the driveway and were about a half-block away when we looked at each other and realized that we'd forgotten Steve. He was still in the house! I guess we were not used to being parents and, just as many young people with a new family, it took us a while.

My last year as a teacher/coach at Star Spencer would occur in the fall of 1968, and spring of 1969. I had felt more comfortable as a teacher in my second year, and as head baseball coach at Star, we succeeded in reaching the finals of the State Baseball Tournament. However, there would be an opportunity available that would give my small family a chance to get back to our original home turf, in Tulsa.

It came to my attention that there was a teacher/coaching position that became available in Tulsa. When I heard of the opportunity, I interviewed and accepted a position as the new head basketball coach at Bishop Kelley, a private Catholic high school. It would be an exciting challenge, and being back home was a bonus.

We'd thought about moving back home to Tulsa and, luckily, it was the right move. With Carol and her family being Catholic, we felt that Bishop Kelley was not only a head coaching opportunity, but it was also the kind of school we'd want our boys to attend. Years later, when they were ready for high school, that's what occurred.

I immediately found that there would be a stark difference between Star and Bishop Kelley. As far as discipline and academics were concerned, my life became a little easier. In athletics, our basketball players worked hard and had a fighting attitude, but it seemed to me that they'd not had much coaching, in the past. After a few weeks in a new system, they were much improved, and developed an intense desire to compete, to win.

The Catholic Brothers who taught and ran the school were great. In my early years, and being around adults who were strict Baptists that didn't drink or dance, I was a little surprised and amused when I received a welcome gift from the Brothers. When I opened the large gift box, it was a case of Christian Brothers Wine! As I said, I was surprised, but I was also very appreciative. You'd never receive a gift like that from higher-ups at a public school, in those days.

I enjoyed the relationships with the students, players, coaches, and teachers at Kelley. However, after one year, Coach Allen had his principal at Webster offer me a teaching, administration, and coaching position, at my old alma mater. It was too good not to accept. At Kelley, I'd had five academic classes with three different subject areas. That meant that there was a great deal of teaching preparation. Trying to coach at a high level and uphold the excellent academics at

Kelley was a difficult task. At Webster, I would become an administrative assistant for attendance each morning, teach one class, and then go to athletics for my sporting assignment. Like I said, I couldn't pass it up.

Those three years at Webster would be an opportunity to work under my mentor, Coach Allen, and learn a great deal more about growing as a coach and teacher. Having grown up on the Westside and now going back to my high school, it seemed a little strange to me but exciting. It had only been eight years since I'd left my old high school days but, now that I was back, it seemed like it was only yesterday.

Right after school began, we would soon have our second son Tim, who was born two years to the day that Steve had arrived. September 29th has always been special because of my two sons being born on that day. My time at Webster had gotten off to a great start, personally, and professionally.

When I began my new position at Webster, I soon found that we not only some great coaches but some very funny characters. As a coach, and because of budgets, you had to be assigned two sports to coach in Tulsa. A second coaching assignment would take me into a new area of coaching. For the first time, I would not just be a basketball coach. My latest assignment would also include assistant junior varsity football coach.

Head football coach, Mark Gibson, was a "Good O'l Country Boy" who grew up in Bixby, which was my stomping ground when I was a young kid. He not only welcomed me as one of his football assistants who'd not played football, but he also made me feel comfortable about coaching his young players. In addition, his personality and country humor made me feel like I'd been coaching with him for years. I always recall one story when I think of coach Gibson. While I was coaching a junior varsity football game, it started to thunder and began to rain. I squatted down and fended off the rain with a poncho. When the game was delayed because of lightning, I later said to Mark, "That's why I'm a basketball coach, because it doesn't rain in the gym!"

A few months later, during the basketball season, I was sitting on the bench inside the gym while coaching our junior varsity team. As a coach, it was one of those times when I really couldn't do much to help our team, as we were losing by a significant margin in the fourth quarter. While focused on the game, and my attention was toward the basketball court, I was tapped on the shoulder. I immediately turned around, and it was coach Gibson. As he looked at me and smiled, and with his country twang, he said, "It rains in the gym sometimes too, dudn'it boy?" We both had a good laugh, as he'd gotten me back for my comment that I made the day we'd had lightning and rain, while I had coached his junior varsity football team.

All of the other coaches were a hoot, as well. It was so relaxed and so much fun that I'll never forget those guys and my time at Webster. After three great years at Webster high school with great coaching and teaching colleagues, there was a new opportunity that arose. The new Charles C. Mason high school was opening in Tulsa. Many basketball coaches were trying to become the first head coach of the new school. I felt that I'd had a very good interview for the new position. Even though I had a very good teaching and coaching resume, I was still nervous. However, by being an ex-OU player, having head coaching experience at Kelly, and with Coach Allen's recommendation, I was catapulted into attaining the position as the first head basketball coach at Mason High School. I was very excited.

The first year as Mason's coach was very difficult. Because it was a new school, we did not have one player that had ever played in a varsity basketball game. However, I've always stated to my close friends that I felt that my first year at Mason was my best coaching job, as we only won two games and lost eighteen. However, my assistants Nate Harris, Claud Moutray, Mike McGivern, and I, never gave up. Even though it had been a tough year with inexperienced juniors and seniors, we had the younger players ready for success, the next year

In that following year, our team defeated Coach Allen and his highly ranked Webster team in the Area Tournament finals and went on to qualify and play in the State Tournament. Because of our rebound from the year before, and being a new school that won its way to the State Tournament, my coaching peers chose me as the Oklahoma Coaches Association Basketball Coach of the Year. It was not only an honor for me but also for my fellow coaches and players.

After all the hard work and time that I'd had spent trying to have a successful basketball experience, I still had questions about the future. I found that even though I worked my butt off, and had some success, the salary I was receiving was still the same, which was $11,000 a year. It was fun coaching and improving our team, but I still had some doubts and apprehension about getting our family finances in order.

While working at Webster, I had commuted seventy-five miles each way twice a week, while studying for a Master's Degree at Northeastern State College, in Tahlequah, Oklahoma. By achieving a Master's Degree in Education, I had been able to get a pay raise that we'd needed. However, now that we had two young sons, we would need a further increase in our finances. I questioned if another teacher pay raise was going to be enough, down the road? With a Masters, I thought that, eventually, I might become a high school principal, if I stayed in education.

After much thought, I knew that I needed to try to become a college coach or pursue a different career than education. I finally concluded that the lifestyle and uncertainty in college coaching, and being dependent on the success or failure of college players, wasn't for me.

In the summer of 1975, my time as a teacher/coach was about to end. A new journey was about to take place. I knew I had to make a change, and I was actively thinking of getting out into the business world. As the word got out that I was about to leave teaching and coaching, a football coach at Mason said to me, "Axley, it's tough out there in the real world. If you leave teaching and coaching, you'll be back in a year!" He didn't know it, but deep inside, I took that as a challenge.

A quote from the great motivational speaker, Jim Rohn, comes to mind, as I thought about my next move. He said, "Your life does not get better by chance; it gets better by change!"

11

THE FORK IN THE ROAD

"Ambition is the path to success.
Persistence is the vehicle you arrive in."
Bill Bradley…Senator/NBA Player

As a small child, I dreamed of modern conveniences in a house on a hill while living in the Shack. That didn't mean that most of my life, I always knew what I wanted as my life goals, or what I aspired to achieve. That is as far from the truth as it could have been. However, something was always pushing me to do better. It seemed as if I was, randomly, just going through life and always taking the next step when certain opportunities might present themselves. I guess my goals had been like most people of the '50s and '60s, which were to go to school, get a high school diploma, get a job, get married, and have a family.

In 1970, we bought a house in Broken Arrow, Oklahoma. Looking back on that purchase, it was crazy how I even considered buying a home, because we were still living paycheck to paycheck. I was coaching at Bishop Kelley when one of the coaches walked into the coach's office and said, "I bought a house!" Up until that time, I'd never thought of owning a house, because rent was all I'd ever known. I proceeded to ask a couple of straightforward questions, which were, "Why did you do it, and how did you do it?" The coaching colleague said to me, "Once you get a loan on the house and own it, you can deduct the interest of the loan on your taxes." He continued by saying, "As you live in the house and the value of it increases, you now have equity that you wouldn't have had in a rental house." It started to make a little sense, to me.

The coach then proceeded to tell me that he assumed an FHA (Federal Housing Administration) loan. Well, I can tell you that an FHA loan meant nothing to me. After asking more questions, I began to search for a house I thought I could afford. Luckily, I found a house for sale by an owner in Broken Arrow, Oklahoma, a suburb of Tulsa. I borrowed $1900 from the Tulsa Teacher's Credit Union to assume a government FHA loan of the previous owner, and bought our small three bedrooms and one bathroom house, for $19,000. I had known nothing about real estate, but I just followed what others were doing. I guess that is one of my life lessons, which is never being afraid to ask questions, even though you may feel stupid in doing so.

We were lucky that houses were appreciating by double digits during those times. After a few years, we sold our first house and used the $10,000 profit as a down payment on a more expensive home in Tulsa. Buying that first house in Broken Arrow was a gateway for us to move up to more expensive homes in the future by using the equity we accumulated, each time.

After teaching and coaching for eight years, and looking toward the future, finances again started to become more important for our family. Thoughts of a private school at Kelley and college for my sons was always in the back of my mind. However, I didn't know what else to pursue as an occupation. I'd gotten my B.S. degree from OU and had earned a Master's Degree, which gave us more of a cushion, but it didn't seem to be enough to start saving for the future.

When school was dismissed for the summer, I did earn extra income by running a summer camp pool for the YMCA. As well, I'd take on odd jobs, such as painting a house or painting house address numbers on sides of curbs with my buddy, Mike Pounds. Even though we were painting curbs, we tried to make it fun by having competitions on who could sell the most at our price of $3.00 per house. We both were competitive coaches, even on the curb circuit.

Carol, who had quit as a teacher, started taking care of some of our neighbor's children for income. However, those small attempts at extra income were not going to be the long-term answer. I needed to open my mind on how to do something different, and that was not easy. As a coach and teacher, it felt good to be of help to students and players, and have some success in athletics. I loved the competition and camaraderie with my fellow coaches, and I knew that it would not be easy to give up on my chosen career.

With my mind racing to figure out what to pursue, I heard of a former coaching colleague who had given up his coaching job and moved into private business. John Tatum, a fellow coach at Star Spencer in Oklahoma City, had become a very successful head football coach. Now that I was looking to change my occupation, I reached out to John and asked why he left coaching?

In a sincere way, John said that as a new head football coach of a weak program, he had worked hard to enable his teams to become of championship-caliber. He felt that he wasn't appreciated for all the time, effort, and hard work he'd put into coaching just to make the kind of income he was making. With that on his mind, John walked into his principal's office for a frank discussion regarding his salary. After those very tense discussions and little progress for a raise, he proceeded to let them know that they didn't deserve someone like himself. He then walked out the door. If you knew John, that was his demeanor. He had always been someone who was "straight to the point."

As John began a search for his next occupation, he found himself walking into the Farm Bureau Insurance Company's corporate office in Oklahoma City. As he entered the lobby, he let the receptionist know that he would like to visit with a successful salesperson with their company. The receptionist was slightly taken off guard with his request, but she relented and brought out the Vice President of Sales to visit with John. That person was impressed that John had "cold called" to visit with him. In sales terms, that meant to walk in off the street while not having a formal appointment, and asking to speak to a particular contact in the business. As I found out later, cold calling was the foundation of making a living as a salesperson. Prospecting for new clients and getting in front of those potential customers to tell your story, is the basics of becoming successful in sales.

In describing his challenge of changing careers, John began to describe how his life had changed financially. When he continued to explain his successful transition from coaching, I felt his excitement when he let me know that his income had gone from $12,000 a year to, approximately, $50,000 with Farm Bureau. My jaw must have dropped. I was amazed at the amount of the increase in a short period of time.

John was an OU jock, like myself, who grew up in the small-town community of Heavener, Oklahoma. As I've said, he was straight-forward and had no pretenses when you talked to him. However, the first thing that came to my mind was that if John can make $50,000, I could do it! Many salespeople have heard the phrase, "if he can do it, I can do it," many times. That phrase is the start of self-motivation in sales, if even by accident. That's not the last time I would repeat that mantra, to motivate myself and imitate the success of someone that I admired.

After a conversation about the parameters of the Farm Bureau sales job, and what it takes to succeed, John immediately said, "There might be an opening in Tulsa. If you'd like, I'll see if I can get you an interview?" Through John, an interview with Farm Bureau was arranged in August of 1975, which led me to win an insurance sales position. That new occupation was a start for me in sales, which allowed me to quit my profession, of teaching and coaching.

Because he inspired me to take a step outside of my comfort zone, I owe a great deal to John Tatum. He encouraged me to make a change and not to look back. Later on, John wrote a book, "The Sooner The Better" which outlined his life and how he became one of the top executives with Farm Bureau.

In that September of 1975, I ambitiously traveled to corporate headquarters in Oklahoma City to train and learn about Farm Bureau Insurance products, and more importantly, some basic selling techniques. It was the beginning of a new path in business, in which my high school coaching colleague referred to as, the "real world."

As Yogi Berra, the hall of fame catcher for the New York Yankees would have said, "When You Arrive at a Fork In the Road, Take it." It was a risk, but that's just what I did when I arrived at the fork.

I Took It!

12

OUT OF THE BLUE

A lot of times, really wonderful things that have come my way have come basically, out of the blue.
Stacey D'Erasmo...Author

Being that I was now a novice in a new profession with Farm Bureau, everything was eye-opening. I tried hard to absorb as much information about company products, and how to sell them to customers, as possible.

Farm Bureau is a full-service insurance company but, at the time, it mostly sold various forms of Farm, Homeowner, and Auto Insurance. John had started his business in Durant, Oklahoma, which was more of a rural and small-town community. I was in the city of Tulsa, which had a much different clientele. By being local, it was good for me; however, there was one thing that was different than other agents in my office. The manager in Tulsa wanted me to sell life insurance exclusively. I soon found that there were not many company leads for just life insurance. If any of my prospects were interested in other insurance products, such as auto and homeowners, I would have to distribute those potential customers to other agents in the office. Asking an individual to look at their life and death situation, and paying for it every month, was a much harder sell. I guess that's why I was supposed to be a specialist? Recognizing the challenge, I relied on my instincts that I'd learned from athletics, which was to "attack the challenge." That's just what I did!

I learned as much as I could about how to sell and how to prospect for new clients in a short time. I worked hard by cold calling or following up on the very few leads that were passed on to me. After studying and working the business a couple of months, I started running into those elite life insurance competitors such as New York Life, Metropolitan Life, Banker's Life, and Mutual of Omaha. Those companies were top of the line in helping people with their long-term planning of assets for families. While competing against my competitors, I found how professional they were and how focused their organizations were with their national advertising in the media. Many of those companies were major sponsors of sporting events or weekly sitcom television series. Others had ads in top-notch national magazines. Not only did I find they were much more visual in the media, but their sales professionals made about three to four times what I made on commissions. At the time, it seemed to me that Farm Bureau was just as its name portrayed. It was mostly geared to patrons in farming and ranching communities, and those who had a loyalty to Farm Bureau. That was not good for a city boy who was only allowed to sell life insurance.

My eyes began to open as I worked every day to try to make it in the life insurance industry. Looking at the business and the company I was representing, I started to analyze the situation. I started thinking to myself, "I can do better!" I guess I was smart enough with my new knowledge that it pushed me to pursue another path. I had a conversation with a person that had sold me a personal life insurance policy before I became a salesperson. Ed Gowns, a part-time musician, had been an Independent Insurance agent for years. When I told Ed of my concerns, Ed encouraged me to look into becoming an Independent Agent like himself, which was to be in business for myself. He even offered to let me office with him free of charge, till I got on my feet.

Things started to pop in my head. What direction or what occupation should I pursue? We had taken our teachers retirement money out of our retirement plans that we'd need to pay our bills. I needed to make some decisions soon. It was another heavy time for thinking about what to do next? Do I go back into coaching? It was too late in the school year to do that. Plus, I remembered the quote from a fellow teacher and coach, which was, "Ax, you can't make it in the real world; you'll be back in a year!" With that in mind, I knew that I would not go back.

About a week later, I walked into the office of the Tulsa manager, and I let him know of my decision to leave. He began to try to talk me out of it. He said, "Alan, you have more talent than any life insurance salesperson we've had in this office." You will be number one in sales!" Being the new kid on the block, I thought to myself, "if I'm number one, I'm probably with the wrong company?" The manager tried again as he said, "Alan, here's a prospective lead that just came into the office. Take this lead and let's visit tomorrow when we both have thought more about how to make it better for you." My mind was made up, but I took the lead.

The contact that I was to go visit lived out in the country, on a farm. It was south of Coweta, which is about thirty miles south of Tulsa. When I reached the location, there was a long dirt road leading up to the prospect's house. The house looked like one that I may have lived in at Leonard, years ago. As I drove up toward the house, I noticed that it needed some paint and had a worn looking front porch, with an old dog barking at me.

I stepped out of the car and walked up to the front door dressed in slacks and a shirt while thinking, "What the hell am I doing here?" As I knocked on the door, an older lady in blue jeans and a flannel shirt answered the door. I politely let her know that I was from Farm Bureau, as she welcomed me into her living room. The furniture was older, but it was clean and simple.

I began by introducing myself with small talk and thanked her for getting in touch with our office. After the pleasantries, I proceeded to ask how I could help her? In a shy way, she said, "I don't know much about insurance or anything, but I've heard about those retirement things for older people, I think they call them Key Holes?" In those days, before IRA's or 401K retirement plans, a small business could open a retirement account with an insurance company, referred to as a "Keogh Plan."

Knowing I was leaving my company, but wanting to be professional, I proceeded to present her with some information that I thought she had requested. Taking in the surroundings, I knew she couldn't afford much, so I guided her toward the minimum allowed. To be honest and knowing I was going to pursue a different path of employment, I wasn't a very good salesperson for her situation, I thought.

After our discussion about the program, I started to wind it down and get ready to go back to Tulsa. I could tell she didn't seem to be very excited or close to making a decision. But, just about the time that I thought I should try to shut it down and leave, she asked, "How much did you say you could put into this Key Hole plan?" I replied, "Ma'am, it's called a Keogh plan, it's $100 to begin and as little as $25 a month, up to $7500 per year." She then stared sheepishly at me and said, "Wait here a minute," and left the room. After a short time, she returned, carrying a large size container. As she opened the lid, she pulled out a roll of bills that you might see if someone had just won a fist full of cash in Las Vegas. As she started to count out hundred-dollar bills one at a time, my mouth dropped! The little lady then asked, "If it's tax-deductible, can I contribute that amount each year for a while, and see how it goes?" In a shy and nervous voice, I said, "Yes, ma'am, you can."

This would turn out to be a great life lesson for me that I've never forgotten. **In business, don't ever judge someone by your first impression of someone's life status, or his or her ability to afford what you or your company is selling!**

When I left and traveled away from the farm, I started to think about how much commission I would make on this sale? I selfishly thought that, maybe, I might be pretty good at this? My mind was wandering what to do, now? Then, as if someone was guiding me, a light went off in my head!

When I went back to the office the next day, and I told of my encounter with the little lady, the manager was pleased. He said, "See Alan, you're a natural. You will be number one in the nation one day." With that, I replied, "Jerry, I just found out why I don't need to be in this business." With that, I let him know that I was going to pursue other avenues of employment, and thanked him for the opportunity. With that, I moved on.

Overnight, I realized that I had felt uncomfortable talking to an individual like the little farm lady and thinking of how much commission I would make on the sale. I now knew that asking for money and selling something intangible to individuals or families was not my cup of tea. Don't get me wrong, life insurance is a necessary product, but I didn't have it in me to nourish my needs by trying to sell it.

I was now making another change and, even though I felt it was the correct decision, it was very unsettling. I had a wife, two small children, and everyday family responsibilities. But, I knew that there had to be something better that fits me, and help to provide a better life for us.

Most of the significant moves that had come my way have happened when I took a risk. I've always felt that my Grandma Box and her spirit were guiding me through my life changes. I had thought of her and the Shack when I was visiting that little lady, in the farmhouse. I felt I should have educated her with alternative ideas, rather than just accepting her money.

I now knew that I needed to be open to other things. As I thought about my next move, for some reason, I had a quiet confidence that everything would work itself out. Little did I know that "Out of the Blue," an opportunity would present itself that would take me down another career path!

13

RIGHT PLACE-RIGHT TIME

"Behold the Turtle:
He only makes progress when he sticks his head out."
James Bryant Conant…Educator/Scientist

Every day in the news, we are introduced to individuals with God-given talents they have refined to become exceptional in their careers. However, masses of the population never pursue, search, or even recognize their real gifts. We all have hidden talents, but when you identify those talents and acknowledge them, we then have to have the fortitude to pursue how to hone those gifts. That may not be easy to do, depending on your circumstances.

I can't tell you how many times I've heard someone ask a young person just entering college or the workforce; "What is your major or, what do you want to do in life?" Most do not have an answer, which is about normal. For others, they may have a special gift and are in the hope of becoming a professional athlete, an entertainer, or a dreamer who thinks they're the next Jeff Bezos, of Amazon. However, for most of us, we have to take a step out into the world and hope we are moving in the right direction.

Many times, you may find an opportunity for yourself in something that you love while pursuing a hobby. The hobby later turns in to something that is not only fulfilling, but now you can transition to your hobby full time, and make a living at it.

How does all of this fit it to the journey I took? Well, as with most in the workforce in America, you have to have a little "luck." In reflecting on my background, it seems that luck has followed me around.

I had luck in finding my final career path, but the discovery of my new journey was not just by accident. The majority of my life's work and any success I might have had were, mainly, because I embraced challenges that were outside of my comfort zone. I was scared and unsure, many times, but I would find that attacking certain obstacles or roadblocks would turn out to be worth the challenge.

My final career move would be by being in the "right place, at the right time." Certain contacts played an important role in me discovering my new occupation. I still say that had I known what I know now, and been more studious and cautious, I may not have followed my decisions that molded a new career.

As I was pursuing leaving Farm Bureau Insurance, I was pondering the idea of becoming an Independent Agent. Unexpectedly, I received a call from my old high school coach, Bill Allen. Coach mentioned that he had been contacted by an acquaintance who asked if he knew of anyone who might be interested in a sales position. The company was known nationwide as, Jostens. Coach asked me if I would be interested. Having just left coaching and a different occupation with Farm Bureau, I immediately said, "No, thanks." I let coach know that I was going to become an owner of a multi-line insurance agency, with the help of an insurance acquaintance. In reality, I didn't want to tell Coach that I had doubts about my next move. I guess I didn't want to sound like I'd made a mistake by leaving the coaching profession.

So, that was it. I declined to interview for the Jostens position. I went back trying to figure out how I was going to make it in another business endeavor. In being honest, I did have thoughts of going back to teaching and coaching, if need be. But those thoughts faded.

As luck would have it, a gentleman by the name of George Mitchell called me at home a couple of days after Coach Allen's visit with me. George said, "Alan, I was referred to you by a friend of Coach Allen's, do you have a moment?" I replied, "Of course, any time I'd hear someone say that they were a friend or referred by Coach Allen; I have time to visit!"

In the conversation, George said that he was a recruiter with Jostens and that he was in town looking for a salesperson. He let me know that Jostens was the largest class ring and yearbook company in America. I told him thanks and that I appreciate him calling, but I'd just gone from coaching to a new endeavor. I let him know that it was too soon for me to be looking around again.

George didn't give up. He let me know that the new manager for the Southern Region of Jostens, and himself, were at the Hilton. He asked, "Could we, at least, just meet with you for thirty minutes, we'd love to visit with you?" For whatever reason, or just maybe because I may have felt a need to be wanted, I agreed.

That afternoon, I went to visit with George Mitchell and the new Southern Area manager, Dave Gibbs. George was an older fellow, and Dave was about thirty or so, which was about my age. In the meeting, they proceeded to discuss their company. George began to explain that Jostens had a new Recognition Division and that the sales position had nothing to do with schools, which was Jostens primary business. The new Division would work with companies, associations, and those in need of custom manufactured awards for employee recognition. Even though they tried to explain about the new Recognition Division, I still knew nothing of what they were talking about regarding their products, or how they sold them. During their discussion about the sales position and Jostens, George's story about Jostens seemed to be coming to an end. At that point, he pulled out two genuine NFL Super Bowl Rings. The first ring was for "Mean Joe Green," of the Pittsburgh Steelers, and the second one was for Super Bowl Quarterback, "Bart Starr," of the Green Bay Packers!

George said, "We manufacture the Super Bowl Rings." Being a sports guy, they had my attention! He had me try the large rings on my finger, which almost gave me goosebumps. He then went on to explain that you couldn't buy these rings. The only way to attain one of these rings would be to earn it by winning the Super Bowl. George continued by saying, "Jostens will present that same message to companies and corporations. For an award to mean something within any organization, it can't just be handed out to everyone. The individual or employee must earn the right to be awarded."

George ended his presentation to me by letting me know that Jostens was listed on the New York Stock Exchange, and was one of the largest manufacturers of custom awards in the country. He now had my full attention and could see that I was impressed. I'd never seen a Championship Ring, let alone a Super Bowl Ring. With that, I figured I was now talking to a very reputable company, and not just some small mom and pop outfit.

After more discussion and conversation, George asked me if I would take a short question & answer test. It was a questionnaire that Jostens gave to prospective Independent Sales Reps regarding personality and whether they would fit within their organization. I thought, "What the hell"... Okay!

I took the test. After I finished giving my answers to a multiple-choice type exam, George and Dave thanked me, very graciously, for meeting with them. As I left, I thought to myself that they were nice guys, but I now needed to get back to figuring out my new direction.

The next morning, I received a call from George. He said, "Alan, you did very well on the Jostens comprehensive sales questionnaire. We specifically look for prospective salespeople with athletic backgrounds and or sales backgrounds. You have both, and you scored very high on this test! We'd love to meet with you again." Well, the way George said that to me kind of boosted my ego, somewhat. So, I accepted and told him I'd come back to the Hilton.

In our next meeting, they explained that the Jostens Oklahoma sales territory had zero Recognition Business, at the time. The opportunity was "brand spanking new!" They felt that the Jostens name recognition, and the new direction of selling their manufactured symbolic awards to companies, was wide open for a new salesperson. I would be the first Jostens Recognition representative and would have the responsibility of developing a new concept in the sales territory.

Going into more specifics, George let me know that Dave Gibbs would be my manager, who then proceeded to explain the monetary aspect of the position. I would have a draw against commission, which would pay me $270 a week. They'd take out no taxes because I would be an Independent Businessman and not an employee of Jostens. Little did I know that the first $270 would immediately put me in a hole? That is, it was a draw or loan against future commissions. That meant that I owed what Jostens had paid to me if I did not make enough in sales and commissions to reduce the total amount of the weekly paychecks. Truthfully, I was not very informed on the payment structure, and I guess I was caught up in the moment of a new adventure. I had questions regarding the draw, and I didn't understand the deal. Tentatively, I told them I'd reflect on our discussion and get back with them.

It was not an easy decision. My sons were seven and five years old. It was unnerving because I had just left Farm Bureau, and as a young father and husband, I had a lot of responsibility on my shoulders. It was scary. After Carol and I discussed the pros and cons, I decided to make a decision that would change my family's life for decades. With much thought and a lot of doubts, I took the sales position with Jostens. It was another new adventure.

George Mitchell flew out of Tulsa, while Dave Gibbs stayed to visit with me about the new challenge. While having dinner with Dave that evening, he let me know that Jostens had a New Man Training School scheduled the first week in December, at their plant in Princeton, Illinois. It was now the second week of November 1975. Before he left, I told Dave that I knew nothing about the business or what I'd be selling. I then looked him in the eye and said to him that my family depended on him to train me to be successful. I told him that I would give 100% effort, but I want his full commitment to getting me started in the right direction. Dave promised to do so, and he kept his word.

My mentor, Coach Allen, gave me valuable advice that day in his office, when he said to me, "Alan, work hard and take advantage of the opportunities that may come your way!"

I had an opportunity, Coach. I worked hard and took advantage of it!

The quote at the start of this chapter rang true, in my instance.

This turtle, "Stuck His Head Out!"

14

FORGE AHEAD

*"A ship is always safe at shore, but
that is not what it's built for."*
Albert Einstein...Physicist

Now that I had changed direction again, I had to be open and ready to attain the knowledge it would take to be successful with Jostens. My new perspective was that I had to quickly open my mind to learning how to be an independent businessman and professional salesman. I would now move into the world of selling products and programs to small, medium, and large organizations. Those prospects included not only private and corporate businesses but also associations and the healthcare industry.

One thing in my favor, while entering this new endeavor of selling to businesses and corporations, was my athletic background. The traits and values you learn playing sports are invaluable in life. Many of the characteristics of an athlete are taken for granted. You have to be competitive, be coachable, set individual and team goals, and learn how to win or lose by not letting either one define you. As well, you have to take care of yourself mentally and physically while embracing some of the most important lessons in business, which are; "Overcoming Rejection, Being Persistent, and Never Giving Up!"

KEEP ON, KEEPIN' ON!

The first time I fully realized Jostens was a first-class company was at the New Man School held in Princeton, Illinois. The training introduced the new trainees to the company culture and how to become a successful Jostens sales representative. Fifteen new prospective independent sales reps were attending the school, including myself. The new reps came from different areas of the country, which ranged from New York to California. My impression of those in attendance was that they all seemed to be excited. Just like me, they all were looking forward to the weeklong training, and what would transpire. However, we were all very apprehensive and wondering how the week would evolve.

Al Edwards, a Jostens Vice-President and sales trainer out of New York, would be the one conducting the weeklong sales seminar. I didn't know it at the time, but if you didn't impress Al and others in management during the training sessions, you'd be sent home by the end of the week. I thought I'd been hired when Dave Gibbs and George Mitchell offered me the job, but that was not the case. Two individuals were eliminated from the school during the week for not being very good with their social interaction and communication skills. That was a surprise. I couldn't imagine going back home and having to explain to family and friends that I didn't make it!

Knowing that the sales position was not guaranteed, my competitiveness kicked into high gear. I had to make sure I made it. I was a little nervous at first, but just as in my basketball days, I upped my game and competed to win.

New Man School was the first time I'd had formal professional training on how to sell any tangible product. The insurance business had been to convince families to give up part of their paycheck to buy an invisible life insurance product to be used in the future. The Recognition Division of Jostens was a first-class manufacturer of awards such as rings, jewelry, plaques, engraved note cards, travel incentives, and products custom made for a company, or corporation. Princeton was the jewelry manufacturing facility in which I was given my first introduction to the unique abilities and skill-sets of the employees that produced those custom awards.

In the sales training section of the classes, the introduction on how to get customers to buy from you was to learn "FAB Selling." Breaking down the FAB selling process, "F" is for Features of a product, the "A" is for the Advantages of that product, and the "B" is for the Benefits of the product to the customer. Being from the coaching and teacher profession, the ABC's of selling was a foreign language!

One of my favorite memories of the training was when Charlie Herrmann interviewed me on videotape. He was a Jostens trainer and motivational speaker who gave sales and business guidance to companies and organizations. The interview intended to see how you would react to questions in a casual conversation. Jostens was checking out your personality by having a pro like Charlie help bring out the best communication skills, in each trainee.

There were no YouTube videos or any film on selling that I'd been exposed to in those days. I guess that is why I was so impressed with Charlie Herrmann. He was someone who could motivate you to feel ten feet tall and make you feel confident about the tremendous opportunity that was in front of you. I had no clue about motivational speakers like Zig Ziglar, Earl Nightingale, Jim Rohn, or anyone like Tony Robbins, but Charlie was truly one of those types in the 70's. In listening to one of his presentations, Charlie would have you ready to jump out of your chair and run out to find a customer. I was mesmerized listening to him, and how he conveyed his positive attitude toward each of us, individually.

Toward the end of the training program, Al Edwards commenced to illustrate how many Jostens Independent Sales Reps were very successful, financially. On the last day, they brought in a current Independent Representative for Jostens to visit with us. Chuck Windsor, who was from Wisconsin, was to give us an idea of what it was like when you are on your own and working every day to develop business, in your territory. Chuck, a former wrestling coach, seemed to be just an everyday guy and was very likable. In a polished but comfortable type presentation to us, I was impressed that he was very professional. As Chuck explained his experience at Jostens, I became inspired by his story and looked forward to working on the sales strategy that laid out for us. He talked of his anxiety when he was a new representative at his New Man Training School, and how he had doubts, after being a coach for fifteen years. During his talk, Chuck began getting to the part about what a rep could expect, monetarily. When he mentioned the amount of money, he and many reps were making for themselves, and their family, I was blown away. Some were making $50,000, $100,000 and few over $250,000 or more. For me, in 1975, that was astronomical.

After his presentation to us, I made sure to visit with Chuck. In our visit he let me know that it would not be easy, but he said if I produced $100,000 of new business in the first year. He'd pay for an expensive dinner for my family and me. I took it as a challenge from one coach to another. I was pumped.

As the Jostens New Man School experience came to a close, the new reps all loaded into a van at the Princeton, Illinois facility, and traveled back to Chicago for a flight home. We all were very eager to get started in the business and use the tools we'd learned. After saying goodbye to my new friends, as we were dropped off at O'Hare Airport in Chicago, I was excited as I reflected on the training class and the challenge ahead.

I had some time before my flight back to Tulsa, so I began to inspect the surroundings. I was in amazement, as I toured O'Hare, which was one of the largest and busiest airports in the world. While staring in the windows and smelling the food in restaurants, I stumbled upon a bookstore. It may have been the excitement from the training I'd just gone through, or words by Al Edwards, Charley Herrmann, and Chuck Windsor that had inspired me, but my eyes became affixed on a particular paperback book. The title moved me toward it. It was my first, but not the last in a long list of books that helped propel my progress as a Salesman/Businessman.

15

GET YOUR MIND RIGHT

"Miss a meal if you have to, but don't miss a book."
Jim Rohn...Motivational Author/Speaker

Napoleon Hill's book, Think And Grow Rich, was the cornerstone for many of the modern-day gurus who give motivation seminars. Most all of them have used many of the valuable lessons in his book, as they try to instill those "Success Habits" to their mass audiences. I still have the original book that I bought that day, in December of 1975. Acquiring that book would start me on a path that I would never have imagined.

I used to preach to my fellow sales representatives that I spent an inordinate amount of time at Barnes and Noble to research and read the many books on motivation and selling. I still have many of those early books and notes in my home office. It's interesting when I reflect on the action I took, and where I started my learning process while trying to absorb those past jewels of motivation. Today, inspirational and success stories are at your fingertips on the Internet for each of us to use, as we see fit.

One of my favorite movies of all time was "Cool Hand Luke" with actor Paul Newman. Luke (Newman), a prisoner in a Southern prison chain gang, kept escaping and always getting caught and punished. A famous saying the prison warden said to Luke came out of that movie. In a whiney Southern accent, the warden would say to Luke before he was severely beaten, "Luke, You Gonna Get Your Mind Right?" One of the first things I found that I had to do in my new endeavor with Jostens was to do just what Luke should have done, and that was to "Get My Mind Right!"

My thought process was like most people who grew up in the 1950's or 60's. We didn't understand that a human mind operated as a computer and that it needs to be programmed correctly. We're now taught by every motivational guru to visualize your end goals with a short and long-term plan to achieve those goals, day by day. After I returned home from the Jostens training session, I started to implement the wisdom from motivational and strategic sales books. It was the first time I'd ever had a plan to achieve certain short and long-term goals that were written down on paper, where I could see them, every day.

Up and till I began my journey with Jostens, I can truthfully say, I was scared. Instead of just reacting to my life and taking the next step on whatever was expected, the Jostens sales opportunity forced me to really look at myself and to truly understand that I could be more successful than I had ever imagined. I started to sell for Jostens in January of 1976. As I found, it wasn't the best time to start calling on those new business prospects that had just finished with the holidays. However, as a new salesperson with butterflies in my stomach, I didn't know better. I was psyched up and ready to go!

In the 70's, there were only three basic ways to meet with a new customer. You could call them on the phone, write a letter asking for an appointment and follow up later, or walk in and ask to see a potential customer. As most in sales will tell you, you had to have "balls" to walk in and interrupt a manager or executive at work, and then get them interested enough to listen to your presentation. Today, with all the guards and gatekeepers, you would have about a two-per-cent chance of walking in off the street and getting a successful business interview. Nowadays, the Internet and the communication processes have drastically changed the way to prospect and visit with someone in a company.

I was fearful as I started my journey down a new path as a Jostens salesman, but I was ready for the challenge. Following what I learned in training, I made a list of targeted prospects in my Oklahoma territory. I made a rule for myself that as I wrote a daily task down on my Jostens notepad, I promised myself that I would pursue what was on that notepad, till it was accomplished. After scratching off finished tasks, I moved those action items that remained to the next day, week, or next month. It sounds primitive today with all of the online prospecting software and tools, which allow us to track our progress. But at the time, I was more organized than I'd ever been.

When I began calling on customers in the first part of January, I was used to being a teacher in a classroom and staying inside when the weather was bad. On a cold day with the wind blowing in Oklahoma, the wind chill goes right through you. One of my first selling experiences was making a trip to Oklahoma City, to prospect for customers by walking into their offices, without an appointment.

It was a dark and damp day as I walked the streets in OKC, and the cold winter wind was filled with snow flurries. After finding a parking meter downtown and carrying a case full of award samples, I began "cold calling" and asking to visit with a potential prospect, one after another. I was dressed in a suit that was a little too large, and I didn't have a suitable overcoat to keep out the wind. To make matters worse, because of the cold, it seemed as if I was the only person on the streets of OKC. I kept asking myself, in a bit of self-pity, "What the hell am I doing in this business?" I'd been a respected teacher and the Oklahoma Coaches Association Coach of the Year in basketball last year. I'm now a sales guy walking the streets in freezing weather with a cold wind that's blowing up my butt, and through my cheap suit coat!"

I had a lonely feeling that day. But after a short time, I snapped out of my self-deprecating attitude. I again remembered what my old coaching colleagues had said to me, which was, "Ax, you'll not make it in the real world, you'll be back to coaching in a year!" Again, that statement was always in the back of my mind, so I pushed on.

After walking the streets of OKC all morning, I finally got a potential customer to talk to me late in the afternoon at Oklahoma Gas and Electric Utility Company. He was very cordial, but he let me know they were happy with the company in which they'd been buying their awards, and didn't look to change. Because he was somewhat friendly, we started to discuss sports, his hometown, and various other topics, plus I needed to stall and stay a little longer in his warm office. Finally, I thanked him and let him know him that I was meeting with Kerr McGee Oil Company, which was about four blocks away. But, in the back of my mind, I was dreading walking out again into the cold winter streets. The OG&E prospect inquisitively looked at me and said, "Are you taking the tunnel?" With a surprised look, I asked, "Tunnel?" He said, "You don't know about the tunnel system?" Evidently, I had not. With that, the gentleman walked with me down to the lobby from an upper floor where we took an elevator to the basement.

After what seemed like five minutes with the OG&E prospect in the elevator, we arrived at the basement level, and the door opened. Low and behold, there was a beautiful and modern tunnel that was carpeted and had decorated walls with street signs that showed directions that connected all the major downtown buildings. But, best of all, it was heated! I was not only astonished and felt stupid, but I sheepishly thanked him as I took off down the tunnel while reading the street sign directions. As I was walking, I started to hear many voices and sounds of activity. To me, and in amazement, it seemed that all of the downtown city was in these tunnels. There were some restaurants and shopping areas crowded with people as they merrily were going about their business. It was just as if we were above ground in the summertime. My attitude changed pretty quickly. I had started to kick myself for feeling sorry for myself, but now I even stopped to have hot chocolate, and browse in a bookstore.

I found that this early selling experience would be one of the first lessons I would learn when prospecting. From then on, I was going to do a little more research before I jump in the car and go calling on companies.

Of my many years in business, I'd learn many lessons similar to the Oklahoma City story. However, it was not the lessons that I learned about sales strategy that was the most important aspect of the selling process. I learned that various business relationships were the essential ingredients in my efforts to succeed. Many of my loyal customers became my "friends in business." Those relationships were the backbone of any of the successes that I achieved, over the years.

The road I took by taking a chance with Jostens while receiving a dismal $270 a week was the start of a better life for my family. Jostens also afforded me the privilege of gaining friends and acquaintances all over the U.S., that I would never have encountered. One of the most important motivators of my selling career was being around other successful sales reps. Later in life, my sons would also have the opportunity that was afforded to me and have taken their business experience to a much more sophisticated and higher level than I ever imagined, for myself.

In 2001, after many years as an Independent Rep with Jostens, the Recognition Division would be sold to a very successful businessman and former coaching friend, Dave Smith. As VP of Sales with MTM Recognition, Dave gave me the responsibility of managing the Independent Reps who came from Jostens, during the acquisition. The experience of working with Dave, and becoming a partner with the MTM family, was an added highlight of my sales adventure.

The major goals I'd written down on paper in Dec. 1976 had come to fruition, many times over. From those first childhood dreams with my Grandma in the Shack, my dreams were fulfilled. Most importantly, it was the journey and the real-life experiences with family, friends, and acquaintances, for which I'm forever grateful.

As the famous poet C.S. Lewis said, "You are never too old to set another goal or dream a new dream." I'm now on a new journey and setting new goals while programming myself for new adventures.

SECTION TWO
PERSONAL REFLECTION

16

THE SALESMAN

Sales are contingent upon the attitude of the Salesman,
not the attitude of the Prospect.
W. Clement Stone…Author/Businessman

I guess by being a businessman and salesman, I've always been interested in the techniques and ingenuity of the profession, and how it has developed over the years. I love the evolution and the way a salesperson has had to adapt to promote their idea, product, or programs, to make a living. As simple as it sounds, and as I've relayed to others who enter the profession, a salesperson is included as part of the top five percent of earners in America. I always follow that statement with a question during any discussion, which is, "If it is true that salespeople are listed as one of the highest monetary professions, why isn't most everyone doing it?" When I get a puzzled look, I follow up by saying, "Because it is hard!"

Most of those in society do not like negatives. In sales, you are going to get a great deal of "no thanks," which most sales individuals take as personal rejection. Rejecting you as an individual is not true ninety-nine per-cent of the time, but it can deflate a person's ego and diminish their self-image if it happens repeatedly. In this day and age, you can use different methods to try to visit with a prospective customer personally, but in my early teens and into early adulthood, it was a very different story.

In the late 40's, 50's, and even in 60's, door-to-door salespeople were walking up to your house or dwelling without previous notice, and asking if you would listen to their "product sales pitch." They were usually selling products for households that were the latest ideas and innovations in the marketplace. An early experience is one that I'll always remember.

One afternoon, a sales guy knocked on the front door of my apartment. He was dressed in a loosely fitted suit and seemed to act like he knew me. After some cordial small talk, he asked if he could show me something revolutionary that he had in his large case. I hesitantly agreed. After him entering and unpacking the case, I soon agreed to listen to his "pitch," or sales presentation, for a Filter Queen Vacuum Cleaner.

Being twenty-two years of age, I'd heard and seen these types of salespeople on television. By being well educated in the ways of the world, I knew I wasn't going to buy any product from a sales shyster who walked up to my door. With that in mind and with quiet confidence, I had decided that I was going to listen to him...for entertainment purposes!

As the salesman proceeded to start his demonstration, the first thing he said was, "I want to show you something astounding!" With a swift hand motion, he proceeded to scatter thumbtacks across my carpet. I was kind of surprised, at first, but as he used the hose of the sweeper to pick the tacks up quickly, I'd made up my mind that I was not going to be impressed. He then looked at me with a slight smile and waited for me to say something. My impression of the attempted demonstration was okay, but I had decided in advance that I was not going to be interested. If that was all he had for me, I was ready for him to go.

After not getting much approval from me on his first demo, he proceeded to place some steel type marbles, or steel balls, about three-quarters of an inch in diameter on the carpet where the tacks had been vacuumed. To my amazement, the machine sucked the steel balls very quickly up the hose, and into the vacuum tank. I wasn't ready for that, and I'm sure he quickly noticed the surprised look on my face. He then looked at me and said, "Just think what this machine can do with ordinary dirt on your floor, or in your carpet?" I now listened a little more intently, while knowing full well that I wasn't going to buy his B.S. However, I was now slightly impressed as he continued with his presentation. The salesman went on to explain that the New Filter Queen was far better and less expensive than the much advertised Kirby Vacuum, which was known as the "King of Sweepers" used by Lucy, on the I Love Lucy television show.

He now had my attention, which made me want to ask, "the question?" As he smiled and waited silently with patience, I finally gave in and asked, "How much does one of those expensive sweepers cost?" I had been curious that he hadn't mentioned the cost, even though I was definitely not going to purchase his product.

After picking up some steel metal pieces again, he looked directly at me in a sincere way and, while reading my body language, waited for my verbal reaction. Finally, I weakened and broke the silence. I said, "Okay, that was impressive, but I'm sure I can't afford it!" He then gave me a reassuring smile and said, "Alan...I can call you Alan, can't I?" I responded confidently, "Sure, that's okay." He said, "The price of this revolutionary machine is $149.00!" I now felt a little relieved because I now knew that I'd outlasted his sales pitch. I immediately and confidently said, "I'm sorry, but that's more than I can afford!"

The salesman was now ready to set the hook! He looked at me in and said, "Alan, what if I could provide this amazing machine to you and your family, "Free of Charge?" I must have had an inquisitive look on my face, for sure, because he was getting closer to my weakness when he said the word...Free! He then said to me, "You seem to be a social type person, Alan. Do you have fifteen friends and acquaintances?" To make sure he knew that, in my mind, I was a macho jock type popular guy, I immediately said, "Sure, absolutely!" He then proceeded to say, "Tell you what I can do. If you set up a presentation for fifteen of those dear friends of yours, I'll give you ten dollars for each one who visits with me regarding the benefits of this Amazing Machine!" He then followed with the closer when he said, "That's $150.00, and would pay for your sweeper!" For me, in the 60's, that was a good deal of money.

To make a long story shorter, I had to pay the $149.00 upfront. I then started contacting my friends to encourage them to watch the salesman's presentation so that I could get reimbursed toward the cost of my sweeper. I found that my good friends were much smarter than me by saying, "screw you, Axley...we don't need no sweeper, and we got better things to do than listen to some sales guy you'd recommend!" I laughed, as I realized that my jock buddies weren't as loyal to me, as I had thought.

So, I learned a life lesson. Don't be so stupid as to try to screw your friends after you'd been sold a "bill of goods." Plus, there ain't Nuthin...Free!

This may also be why I have had success as a salesman for over forty years. I've always had to remember that to be successful; it's the attitude of the salesman, and not the attitude of the "prospect"... as I had been.

Lastly, the sweeper could pick up thumbtacks and steel balls, but it never could pick up dirt!

17

FRIENDS

'That's right, I stepped up!
She's my friend, and she needed help.
If I had to, I'd pee on any one of you!"
Joey...Friends/TV Series

The quote above is from "Friends," a television comedy series, which was one of the most famous sitcom shows of all time. In one episode, there is a scene that is still famous on YouTube. While swimming in the ocean, a jellyfish had stung Monica. As gross as it sounds and whether fact or fiction, the other actor thinks he's helping his friend, and that peeing on the sting will quickly take the pain away. It was just one of the hilarious episodes on the show.

I can truthfully say that I've had loyal friends who would eagerly pee on me to ease my pain. I guess I had some "wild and crazy friends!" I'm positive they'd say that I'd do the same to them.

When I left high school for college, I was apprehensive and a little insecure about leaving my close friends from high school. It was a time that I had to branch out and get out of my comfort zone. It's funny how friendships change when circumstances change. When I started my occupations of teaching, coaching, and sales, I developed many new relationships, repeatedly.

KEEP ON, KEEPIN' ON!

I've realized that there are different levels of friends. Some of our casual friends are acquaintances. There are also inner circles of friends, in which we can confide and talk about common interests, in our everyday lives. Then, some may be your "core friends," who are individuals who know much of your social history and inner feelings. Core friends are almost like a brother or sister. They'll be there for you in a crisis and do their best to come to your aid.

I found that I needed to be open to new friendships, but I didn't automatically think that everyone friendly with you should be considered your friend. It's' good to go through the necessary steps to make sure their friendly intentions are for the right reasons. Even though I've made many friends in business and sports, it seems most of my loyalty is with the ones who came from a similar environment, or with whom I shared most of my difficulties and successes. They were friends that accepted me, even with my faults. Mostly, they've had similar experiences, socially and economically, with me.

I was fortunate to bond with many of my teammates at OU, with whom I shared athletic successes and failures. We weren't always the best citizens by using our jock mentality, but we respected and looked out for each other, as we meandered our way through various challenges.

You can usually count your loyal friends on the one hand. I have to mention a couple of my long-time friends.

Freddie Hensley was the fourth of five brothers. He was a good friend that I grew up within the 50's and 60's that turned in to a best friend. Even though he was a pretty decent athlete in baseball, football, and basketball, Freddie was known for pushing the envelope, socially. As teenagers, he was one of the first to educate some of us boys into thinking about girls. If you saw any of the movies where there was a guy who was kind of on the edge of raunchy, such as in the movie Porky's, or saw a flick about a funny guy trying to score with a chick all the time, that was Freddie in high school.

I'd be lying if I said Freddie didn't have an impact on my friends and me. We were exploring our sexuality as teenagers and Freddie had the guts to talk to girls in a teasing kind of way. Most everyone in our old high school group has a "Freddie Story." I will confess that I can't put all the blame on Freddie, for some of the wild antics of my peers and me. As teenagers, my buddies and I were very inquisitive, as we pursued many "mischievous and youthful indiscretions."

After graduating with a Masters Degree in Petroleum Engineering from the University of Tulsa, Fred became very successful in the oil business. Many of my close friends and former classmates would say, who'd a thought it?

We can now say, "Freddie showed us!"

Recently, Freddie has been in ill health but is still as playful and ornery as he has always been. It was fun to see him being a playful and, somewhat off-colored grandpa, while his grandkids were visiting him in the hospital. It was the same, Freddie. He was still cracking jokes while laying flat on his back, trying to recover from a health issue.

Mike Pounds, another high school friend is another best friend. Mike was a successful former basketball coach that eventually retired as an administrator with the Tulsa Public Schools. Mike is the friend that will be there for you in good times to celebrate, and in bad times to help you cope. He's at his best when you need a confidant you can depend upon. Mike is a very family-oriented person, and you know that he truly cares about you by his actions.

In describing Mike, one of his most important personality traits is "trust!" When I say trust, I emphasize that I mean trust with your thoughts and feelings. You don't always share those closely-held events or long-held descriptions of your past to someone, without them earning your trust. Those hidden inner thoughts should not be shared easily. In my adult years, Mike has always been there for me. In return, I would do anything I could to help him.

The difference in my relationship with those two life long friends is as follows:

Should a jellyfish ever bite me, these two would react the same way. They'd both like to pee on my sting to relieve the pain, just as Joey, of the sitcom Friends, did for Monica. While trying to stop the pain, Freddie would pee on the sting in retribution of some past event between us, and laugh about finally being able to get even. However, all the while, he still had the good intention of knowing that his gesture was going to help me recover from the sting.

Being that Mike is a problem solver and an action-oriented type of guy, Mike would pee on the sting, as well. But it would be to make sure I was not going to be in any more pain, period. Mike's enjoyment would be to help in an emergency and bring the problem to a positive conclusion. He's always been good at solving problems. After the emergency was solved, we'd both have a good laugh at how in the hell did I let a jellyfish catch me, in the first place? I proudly call Freddie and Mike, my friends, and… my brothers!

Maurice Claret was a very successful Ohio State football player and potential multi-million dollar professional football player. He began to run with the wrong crowd and had to serve a prison sentence. He's had various seminars and generally speaks to young men about their choices in life. During one visit with a group of young adolescents, an inner-city youngster asked Claret a pointed question? "Mr. Claret, what is the one piece of advice you would give to me, personally?" Claret answered very quickly. He said, **"show me your friends, and I'll show you your future!"** I felt that the answer was profound!

Most of my friends have been successful in their life adventures. Whether on purpose or sometimes accidentally, I picked and associated with those who wanted to work and succeed in their chosen journey.

I feel lucky to have had the close friendships that had an incredible influence on me, for which I am so very thankful.

There is no doubt that if they ever needed me, "I'd Pee On Em!"

18

FEAR

"We fear beginnings; we fear endings. We fear changing; we fear staying stuck. We fear success; we fear failure. We fear living; we fear dying."
Susan Jeffers…Author

Many noted scholars in psychology say the first few years of a child's life can determine the foundation of how they will participate in their new game of life. Some clinical psychologists have said that we hold early emotional feelings of love, fear, and survival throughout our lifetimes.

Being that I came from a poor background, as well as, not having the best family environment, I find much of my success or failure was determined by how I reacted to fear. I've loved the quote by Scottish author Paul Sweeney that rings true to multitudes of those who are trying to move out of their comfort zone. I know it did with me. Sweeney said, "True success is overcoming the fear of being unsuccessful." None of us want to fail. Many times, we give up when we are right on the cusp of reaching our goals, because of our fear of not succeeding.

Most psychologists would try to explain people's reactions to fear in the following manner. They would probably say that we react to internal or external fear just as an animal would react, which is Fight or Flight! You attack fear, or you run away from it. I've done both.

Whether it was fear of not fitting into various social situations, fear of uncertain family circumstances, or the fear of failure in business, I concluded that the best way for me to get through my anxieties was to "take action!"

As an adult in business, I can recall walking around a building three or four times with butterflies in my stomach before calling on a potential business customer. As a teenager, whether it was trying to make an athletic team, asking a girl on a date, or fear of failing in school, fear was always in the background.

In business, coaching, or a marriage, there was always the fear of not being good enough. Even when I would receive a positive accolade for the achievement of a well-planned accomplishment, I sometimes felt that I didn't deserve whatever level of success that came to me. In those times, I couldn't put my finger on why I acted or reacted to any of my fears of failure. Any sub-conscious experience that may have had any influence on my present thoughts or behavior wasn't even on my radar.

While trying to discover and analyze my feelings, I held most of my fears close to the vest. Loved ones, friends, or acquaintances may not have picked up on my fear, but it was always in the background.

Thankfully, I ran across a book that seemed to explain and help me to understand what I had instinctively been doing all my life. The title was "Feel The Fear and Do It, Anyway, by Susan Jeffers." I probably had been "feeling it" and "doing it anyway" all along, but I didn't understand overcoming fear as a strategy. I assume I was mostly in survival mode when faced with difficult challenges, so I instinctively attacked the situation.

While trying to overcome any insecurities and different paths that I've taken, I started looking in the mirror and pursued becoming honest with myself, many times. When I asked myself a very direct personal question about my feelings or actions, it wasn't always easy to give an honest answer, while starring back in that mirror. But, I can say that when I kept the "mirror" exercise simple; by telling the truth to myself, it was eye-opening!

To have courage and overcome any fear and uneasiness when faced with a challenge, I always looked at those who were successful and tried to emulate some of their positive traits, as they attacked their challenges.

Whether it was instinct or survival, I followed the pattern verbalized by WFC Female Champion Fighter Rhonda Rousey when she said, "You Have To Have Fear, In Order To Have Courage."

I am proud to say that I've had some Courage!

19

FAMILY

"Families are like branches on a tree, we grow in different directions
yet our roots remain as one."
Unknown

How many times have we heard someone who has just completed a successful team challenge say, "We're like family!" I've had that feeling many times in sports and with my business colleagues. However, when it gets down to it, it's not like most families.

In reality, the above quote is about our personal families. In the 50's, it would have been Ozzie, and Harriet or Father Knows Best, who would be considered a "functional family." Their television lives never saw serious challenges that can occur while raising their studio family.

In today's soap operas on television and movies, we tend to get a great deal of drama depicting dysfunctional families trying to overcome adversities, in everyday relationships. Many of those are far too negative, and way overdone.

I recently read an article by an author who wrote that there are two types of families. The first is the one we are born with, and the second is the one you acquire. I've found that recognizing your faults from a born family can be difficult. As adults, we tend to cling to certain behaviors and values that we grew up with in the past, even though many of those traits are carried subconsciously. I'm sure that was a partial reason for some of my difficulties.

The family in which I was born was poor and had lived a rural type of life during the 1930s and 1940s. The norm for them was one of survival, which was food, clothing, and shelter. As an adult, I carried many of those earlier family traits into my everyday personal and business life. Fear of poverty by working hard to overcome any lack of financial stability was always in the back of my mind. Another trait from my early ancestors was an emotional trait of not verbally expressing feelings of love, enough. Love of family was assumed or taken for granted.

In my adolescent years and as a young adult, those my age would marry in their late teens, or shortly out of high school. Because of a high school sweetheart or someone they dated over time, it seemed the next step was marriage and a family.

At the age of seventeen, I met my future wife, Carol, through a blind date set up by one of my basketball teammates. At the end of our senior year in high school, Carol and I dated before we went off to college. We kept in touch via mail and continued to date during summer vacation and various college breaks. After having left school after a couple of years in college, Carol came back to Tulsa from the University of Southern Mississippi, and we started to date, even more. Long story short, we were married in the summer of 1965 before my senior year in college. My basketball buddies and their girlfriends became our close family friends. While I played basketball and took the classes I needed to graduate, Carol worked for the University while attending classes to finish her degree.

Being a young man and having started a marriage, I'd had no training for a typical family life. I felt that I would have to depend on Carol's experience to bring what she'd known with her family, into our lives. Being around the Cumiskey family, I felt part of something that I perceived as normal, and one that you'd see on television. I felt that Paul and Betty, Carol's parents, made their best effort to make me feel accepted, as their son-in-law.

As for what I could add to building the characteristics that we needed, I tried to contribute what I knew to make our family successful, and that was to work hard. Early in marriage and when we didn't have funds to fix things, I figured it out. I did the "manly" chores that were expected, even though I'd had no hands-on training. As far as raising children, I tried to give my sons the best of what I'd learned and what I was proficient at in life, which were sports and business. Above all, I wanted them to feel secure in their home environment, as they grew from youngsters into young adults.

Our family was functional most of the time. But, like most families, Carol and I had disagreements over various parts of marriage and responsibilities. I give Carol credit for trying her best to keep us grounded. In all honesty, I believe that I was so busy trying to graduate, make a living, and later become successful in any way I could, that I was not a good husband.

Someday, I hope that Carol and I can look back together and be proud of all the positive experiences we enjoyed with our family. We had some great times and raised two outstanding and successful sons.

After being single for over twenty years, I became part of a new family when Stacey Gray and I were married. I'm definitely a much different person. Being much older, I've found that I'm able to express my emotions and feelings of love, more openly. As well, by Stacey having Canines when we dated, Halo and Lulu welcomed me into their family. They have since passed away, but I learned so much from them about loyalty and unconditional love. Rosie, our one-year-old Canine, is a new addition to our family. She is beautiful, energetic, and full of life. She contributes to helping both of us feel much younger. The phrase in the first paragraph of this chapter rings true for us; "We're like family."

Family is the core of what makes a community, a country, and the world function. The love and loyalty of a family is a bonus in this day and age. Sometimes there are bumps in the road, and we fall.
When we stop and assess our situation, it is usually loyalty and the love of family that drives us, to get back up!

20

FORGIVENESS

"When you forgive, you in no way change
the past-but you sure do change the future!"
Bernard Meltzer...Radio Personality

I never really had a connection with Cecil, my father. I can only recall a few alone times with him when I was young. Even when he remarried my mom, he wasn't father material and didn't spend much time with my brother and me.

One day, after thirty years of him being out of my life, he briefly appeared. On my way to a business meeting, I started to exit from an expressway, close to downtown Tulsa. As I looked toward the shoulder of the road, I noticed a man with a strange walk. As a very young kid, I remembered that Cecil had walked with his toes outward, almost like a duck would walk. As I drove close to him and looked his way, I knew it was Cecil.

I first said to myself, "No, I won't pick the asshole up." But, for some reason, I immediately changed my mind and pulled over to the side of the expressway in front of him, and waited for him to walk up to my car.

I think the reason I stopped was that I'd just gotten through a counseling session the week before, regarding forgiveness. I'd gone to a group session to work on personal events, in hopes of having a better marriage. The group session was a great experience in learning about some of the past garbage in my life.

When I picked him up, I noticed he was wearing a worn flannel shirt and dirty pants, as well as a weathered John Deere cap. As he opened the back door of my car, I said "Where ya going?" He replied, "I'm headed downtown." I immediately replied to him, "Get in, I'll take you." It wasn't a great distance to the center of Tulsa. It was maybe ten or fifteen minutes via the expressway.

As I looked over my shoulder and inched my way safely into traffic, I said to him, "Do you know who I am?" In which, through his white scraggly facial hair, he replied, "No, I don't?" I nervously responded, "I'm Alan, your son!" In my rearview mirror, he looked a little puzzled and said, "You're a big O'l Boy!" I had a negative feeling emerge at the time, as I thought to myself, "You damn right, I'm a big boy, all 6'6" inches of me. The last time you saw me, I was a kid."

With that, we talked about where he was living or where I should drop him off. He asked me to let him out at the Central Library. I knew that outside of the downtown library was where many of the homeless congregated. As I pulled in front of the library, I slowed the car to pull close to a curb, directly across the street. A few homeless guys were relaxing on wooden benches and others leaning on a red brick border fence, in front of the building. The weather was great, and all of the men seemed to be taking advantage of it.

As I stopped the car, Cecil got out of the back seat and stepped up on to the curb. I decided to get out of the driver's side and walk around to say something to him. Then, almost instinctively, I pulled a fifty-dollar bill out of my wallet. I don't know why, but I guess I felt that he was a poor homeless guy, and it was the thing to do? As I glanced at his face to say goodbye, it seemed as if our eyes met at the same time. Again, not knowing how to act or react, I started to tear up as I swallowed and felt a lump in my throat. I then hugged him as I inserted the money and a business card into his hand. When I hugged him, he hugged me back and told me thanks, and that he appreciated it.

As I left, I noticed the transients across the street that had been looking our way. I'm sure they were thinking, "why in the hell is this guy in a pinstriped suit hugging this typically dressed transient while standing in front of a late model automobile?" I'm sure it looked a little strange, to them. But, I felt good that I'd given Cecil some cash.

After that encounter, I saw Cecil two more times. My feelings of anger had started to fade after the first meeting. About two or three weeks later, he called and wanted me to meet him at the Denver Grille Café, where many of the homeless guys hung out in downtown Tulsa. He wanted to give me some money back for the fifty I'd given to him earlier when we first met.

I did go to see him. I thought that this would be as good a time as any to use my forgiveness training and to let go of any hard feelings or anger that I'd held from my past. As I entered the small restaurant, it seemed that everyone knew Cecil. The lady that owned the downtown Denver Grille seemed happy to see me, as Cecil proceeded to introduce me as his son to her and all the fellas sitting at the counter, and in the booths. The little cafe' had a mixture of what looked like blue-collar patrons, and some transients.

After a short time in the small café, Cecil offered me twenty dollars. I don't know where he got it, but it seemed that he wanted to pay me back, in some way. He insisted, so I took it to make him feel good about his offer. Before I left the restaurant, I gave the twenty that he'd given to me, and some additional cash, to the owner. I asked her to pay for Cecil's food anytime he came in to eat, or order, and she graciously agreed. She seemed to be one of those individuals who wanted to help others, especially her regulars.

As I started to leave, I asked Cecil to follow me outside for a visit. When outside, I pointed to my car and invited him to sit shotgun on the passenger's side. He got into my car, as I entered into the driver's side entrance. As I looked at him, he was weathered, scruffy, and somewhat smelly, but he seemed to smile and be very confident.

Being that I'd just been through the group counseling session the month before, I was going use my knowledge to communicate with this guy who had not been a father to me for most of my life. I wanted to tell him of all the times my mom, my brother, and I had struggled, financially. Even though we'd never heard from him or received any support, I wanted him to know that we made it. We were all okay!

Now that we were in the car, it seemed like an hour had passed, as I tried to get my thoughts together. I'm sure that I still had some hidden anger after all of those many years, but I was ready to let it go. After I took a deep sigh, I said, "I'd like to tell you something." Looking at me with a slight smile on his face through his unshaven and gruff beard, he said, "What's that?" I said to him, "I just want you to know that I forgive you." Cecil didn't hesitate with his reply as he looked at me in a puzzled way? Then, came his response. "For what?"

I don't know what I'd expected, but I sat there for a second without answering, a slow smile emerged. I thought this man had lived most of his entire life in his environment and seemed satisfied with his life. He was at peace with how he had lived his life. I was someone who had not been in his life for thirty or more years. I now understood; Cecil had moved on, long ago!

Outside the small café that day, I realized that I didn't forgive my father to make him feel better. I did it for me. I was okay with his answer, and I now understood that I could leave our history of dysfunction in my early years, and go on without resentment. It was refreshing. I had come to realize that it had been a waste of time to hold on to the past.

"To forgive is to set a prisoner free; and discover the prisoner was you."
...Unknown

21

FATHER & SON

"It is not flesh and blood, but the
heart, which makes us Fathers and Sons."
Friedrich Schiller…Poet / Playwright

As I left the little restaurant, after meeting Cecil and his friends, it felt good. It was a great day. Periodically, over the next few weeks, I left some money for him with the owner of the Denver Grille. But, we still led two different lives. He was an older, alcoholic homeless person who seemed to be okay with his plight in life. I was raising a family and trying to be successful in a challenging business.

In a busy summer of 1989, I was still building my business, but I also was involved with coaching an AAU All-Star Basketball Team. I'd been away from Tulsa for a couple of weeks with our team in July, and it was now early August. It was when I was getting back home from the basketball tournament in Phoenix when I heard that the Osteopathic Hospital in Tulsa wanted me to get in touch with them. When I did contact the admissions office, they let me know that Cecil Ambrose Axley had been in the hospital for a month, and was in a coma. They explained that he'd been in a skirmish and had gotten an injury. They didn't know any of the specifics of how he'd gotten hurt, but they quickly let me know that they'd been searching for the closest relative.

When I arrive at the hospital, I didn't know what to expect. As I approached the waiting area, the nurse at the main desk told me that a doctor would meet me in a family waiting room, on a certain floor. As I entered the area, the doctor was waiting for me. He let me know how very glad he was to see me, and that the hospital had been trying to find the closest next of kin for Cecil Axley, for about a month.

After the short introduction, the doctor let me know that Cecil was on a breathing machine and that the prognosis was not good. He informed me that his heart was beating and he had a few body functions, but that he was brain dead. I can honestly say that I was shocked. I wasn't expecting that, at all. I wasn't ready for that kind of news.

After digesting what I'd just heard, I hesitantly walked into Cecil's hospital room. My first impression was that you could tell they'd shaved his beard, and he looked a lot cleaner than the last time I'd seen him. As I looked at his wavy white hair that was groomed and combed, I thought of how his hair looked a great deal like mine. As the doctor began to explain the situation, I had my eyes affixed to Cecil and all of the medical equipment attached to him.

The doctor then proceeded to be direct and let me know that there was no chance of him recovering. As the doctor kept talking, and even before I could absorb the situation, I could tell he was trying to get me to a point to go further with the conversation. It's as if he'd been waiting for a long time to visit with someone who might be responsible for Cecil Axley. The doctor looked at me and proceeded to ask a question that caught me off guard. He said, "Being that you are the closest next of kin, I need your help? I need your permission to unhook the ventilator from your father." Earlier, he had assured me that the machine was the only thing keeping Cecil Axley alive, as oxygen was pumped into his lungs and distributed throughout his body. I was shocked! It was almost like a punch in my stomach. In no way was I ready for that gut-wrenching request.

After I calmed my thoughts, I looked at the doctor, and all of a sudden out of my mouth, it came, "What? Are you asking me to be the one to take him off this machine? I hardly know this man. I've not been around him but two or three times in thirty years." The doctor explained that he hated to put that responsibility on me, but I was the closest relative. I said, "I have an uncle or aunt who is much closer to him than me?" In which he replied, "Because you are his son, it falls upon you to make the decision." I was kind of in a stupor. I guess the one word that described my feeling was that I felt "overwhelmed!"

After I had time to regroup and collect my thoughts, I told the doctor that I'd have to think about our conversation, I couldn't make that kind of decision right now. I followed with another response. I told the doctor that if I did agree to take him off the ventilator, I'd have to be positive and that I wanted another brain scan for certainty. He agreed and let me know that it would take till the next morning to get it done. I was shaken at what had just taken place at the hospital. I just wanted to get out of there and start to evaluate the situation while getting my thoughts together.

After going home, I concluded that I needed some help. All of our family was Catholic. Sister Sylvia, a friend of the family who was also a nun at our church, was a very down to earth person. I felt comfortable that she could help me with some religious direction. After I explained the situation to her, she agreed to meet me the next morning at the hospital.

When I met Sister Sylvia that next morning, we went immediately to the hospital room. Cecil had already returned from the promised brain scan. The doctor came in the room and advised us that the new brain scan had not changed and that there was no doubt that he was "brain dead." As well, the doctor let me know that Cecil's scans showed very advanced lung cancer in them.

As the doctor left, it was quiet in the room. After a short time and while gazing down at my father, I asked Sister Sylvia what she thought I should do? As she nodded towards him, she said, "Alan, if you were in that situation, would you want to live like that?" I slowly looked into her eyes and, reluctantly, said, "No." Sister Sylvia then asked if she could give Cecil the last rights of the Catholic Church. I replied instantly to her, "Of course!" As I sat and watched while she proceeded with some prayers and started to put some ointment on his face, she said prayers that blessed a person that was in the last part of life. I was feeling helpless. I silently wondered if he'd ever been to church? But, as of right now, there was someone who was blessing his soul, and I felt good about it for him.

Toward the end of receiving the last rights in the hospital room ceremony, I was standing and reflecting over Cecil Axley and thinking to myself, "Here lies my father whom I'd not known, most of my life." It was then that I internally acknowledged to myself that, no matter the past, Cecil was my father. He had his life, and it wasn't what I would have wanted for him, but this was a human being that deserved dignity. I was sincere when I'd said earlier that I forgave him. At this time, he was my blood. It was very difficult for me, as I was having feelings and some personal insight that I'd not expected.

After Sister Sylvia left, I proceeded to let the doctor know that I'd finally agreed to unhook the ventilator. The doctor and nurses started the routine of disconnecting all of the apparatus connected to Cecil. As I sat there with my father, I noticed some tears on his cheek from his eyes, which led me to summon the nurse on duty. When I asked about the tears, the nurse informed me that it was only a tear ducts that were still active to air. But, in my thoughts, it meant that he knew I was there as I rubbed my hand over his wavy white hair. Finally, as the nurses left, and I was standing over him with some tears in my own eyes, I said to him, "I love you."

I knew his life would be over in the next few minutes or hours. I have to say that this next part has had a profound effect on my life. It was something that I'd not shared, except with close friends.

Being alone with my father, I sadly and nervously sat in a chair next to him. As I was reflecting and recalling memories of our short father and son's past, all of a sudden, I felt something strange happening. It seemed as if the air or atmosphere in the room started to become very unsettling, to me. As I gazed at him lying in bed, it was as if something silently moved up and out of my dad's body, which sent chills up my spine. I was never an overtly or devout religious guy but, at that moment, I nervously think I came to understand what had happened. I'm positive I felt my father's spirit leave his body. The more I experienced this event, the more my emotions went from sadness for his physical body, to one of happiness for his new spiritual life. Since that time, I feel blessed to have been there to share that moving and defining moment with him.

My mind was trying to analyze how I was feeling and what had just happened. I was thinking to myself, "here was a guy who many would have thought was a lost soul on this earth, and now my thoughts were of acknowledging and recognizing that he was now in the afterlife, with God." That spiritual experience with him that day has influenced my religious beliefs in a very profound way.

His funeral was a graveside service arranged by my Uncle Art, the owner of a funeral home. Sister Sylvia had arranged for the director of the Tulsa Metropolitan Ministry, a homeless shelter, to give the eulogy. With words such as leadership, respect, compassion, and fun to be around describing Cecil Axley, it opened my eyes even further about the life my father had led in his homeless environment. You'd have not known Cecil Axley was a homeless person. You'd have thought he was a pillar of the community.

I'm so glad that I didn't let my ego keep me from stopping my car and giving this homeless man a ride that summer. The experience led me to have total forgiveness, love, and compassion for a person that was a father I'd never really known.

In my case, the quote by Friedrich Schiller, a German philosopher, rings true. It is "The Heart That Makes Us Father And Son, Not Flesh And Blood."

22

MOTHER AND SON

"Men are what their mothers made them."
Ralph Waldo Emerson...Poet

On a hot Oklahoma day in the first week of August, I was close to the Bixby Cemetery, where my mom was laid to rest. I decided I wouldn't wait till her birthday on August 15, as I drove into the entrance and parked close to her grave.

As I approached her headstone, certain thoughts and feelings started flowing about our journey together, as Mother and Son.

When Mom was eighty-eight years of age and with her, slightly guarded permission, I began interviewing her about her life by asking questions of her past. When I say interview, I wanted to not only know about her impression of her life but also to try to understand and decipher how that past had affected my brother and me, as youngsters.

In visiting about Mom's past, and her having grown up in hard times, I soon drew her into a series of conversations.
She was candid in recalling her childhood and being raised by her grandma and grandpa Hood. One surprise to me was when she explained how she thought that her birth mother was her sister until she was about ten years of age. Her mother, my grandma Barnes, had

children from four different men. Mom had five stepsisters and one stepbrother. My own mom's four short and failed marriages, as well as trying to survive as a single mom while raising two boys, made it difficult for her. I can't imagine what my Grandma Barnes endured.

A big part of my interview sessions with Mom related to families like hers that survived the 1930's, and the war-torn 1940's. In her mind, those times were a period when families had to "buck up" and do what it took to make a living and survive. In describing various segments of her life, most of our discussion always drifted back to the different work environments that she'd encountered.

In Bixby, Mom attended school through the eighth grade. At the age of twelve, she began to work washing dishes at a small local cafe. After her dishwasher job, she began waiting tables in small country cafés, for years. In the late '70s and early '80s, there was a funny television show that kind of reminded me of Mom. The title of the series was called, Alice, and was about waitresses working in a diner. One of the waitresses was a Southerner who was funny and, sometimes, sassy. In short, she did not let a mouthy customer walk all over her. Her famous saying when someone was out of line, or she was questioning what just happened was, "Well, Kiss My Grits!" She was a hoot! That was Mom's demeanor, as a waitress.

During WWII, as many young ladies, she was part of an aircraft assembly line for Douglas Aircraft Company in Tulsa. Because most of the men had gone off to war, females were asked to work as laborers on airplanes, and other military manufacturing projects. Those females that worked helping to build airplanes by riveting them together would later be glorified in our newspapers and on posters as, "Rosie, The Riveter."

After the war, Mom worked on assembly lines for companies, such as, Zebco Rods and Reels and Liberty Glass Plant, in which the men working next to her made much higher wages than she did, as a single female. That definitely would not be allowed in today's workplace environment.

In the 50's, Mom worked two jobs at once when we were in a bind for groceries and rent. I remember her going to work as a waitress from seven in the morning until two in the afternoon and then go directly to her position on a manufacturing assembly line, for the three to eleven evening shift.

As an older adult, she worked in a flower shop making arrangements, as well as delivering bouquets and gifts to recipients all around Tulsa. Work for Mom was not only a necessity; it was in her DNA.

Finally, after all of her occupational experiences, she said she had been fortunate to find her calling in life.

After she'd moved to Tacoma, Washington with her half brother, William, she worked part-time in the cafeteria of a U.S. Army Base, in Ft. Lewis, Washington. That is where she made contact with an Army General and his wife, who needed help from a private caregiver. She took the challenge and ended up caring for them in their home for about four or five years. Over time, the General passed away, and his wife followed by dying a couple of years later. Mom said it was sad to see those you care for come to the end of their lives, but it was worth every bit of the time she spent with them. She said it helped her feel that she was an important part of someone's life.

Some people never find a niche in life's journey, but as luck would have it, Mom had found her purpose. After Mom moved back to Tulsa from Tacoma, she would later move on to what would become her last working experience. She would become a caregiver for an older lady in Bixby, her old hometown. Elsie Ramsey not only became her client, she also became her best friend.

My mom was not known as being overtly affectionate, but as I visited her at Elsie's house a few times, I saw Mom as a person who dearly loved this lady. It truly melted my heart to watch her give love and attention to Mrs. Ramsey. After a few years and having age-related health issues, Elsie died. Mom didn't like to show weakness or display sad emotion, but Elsie's death affected her more than she wanted to admit. In visiting about her time as a caretaker, she was always proud and happy to talk about the days of her and Elsie's time together. After Elsie's passing, Mom always let us know when she'd visited with Elsie's family, whom she'd kept in contact. It made her day when she'd get a card or a call from them.

With her friend Elsie having passed, and Mom getting older, she had felt that she didn't have the stamina to continue her work as a caregiver. She didn't know if she could endure any more heartbreak, should someone lose his or her fight to survive old age. That time spent with Elsie would be the last of her work adventure.

You learn quite a lot visiting with an older parent about their life experience. I learned much more about Mom than I'd expected, during my interview.

At the end of her life, she would tell her friends or anyone who'd listen how proud she was of her boys. She loved what we had as a family. I mention family because even though it wasn't the typical television family, it was our family. Just as single moms today, our mom took on the financial responsibility, as well as, the role of mother and father.

Any struggles she had financially, became me and my brother's struggles, as well. There were times of bill collectors calling us, utilities disrupted because of late payments, and the scarcity of everyday necessities, which brought anxiety and fear into our family. Those fears were real to us all. There were times that I didn't know how she was going to cope with the financial challenges, mentally. But, she always rebounded and recovered, time and time, again.

I feel proud of her fight in those times of difficult relationships, parental responsibilities, and health issues, while always trying to take the next step to make our lives better. Even though she was not school educated, she made sure Tom, and I respected our educational journey. She put us in the hands of teachers and role models that allowed us to prosper in life, through those relationships.

I recall what I'd heard a counselor say to me later in my adult life, regarding parents; he said, "Alan, all families have uncertainties, disappointments and, sometimes, anger toward their parents. But, there is no exact science in raising a family, while trying to meander your way through life. We do the best we can with what we have available to us, at the time."

As I stood alone that August day and visited with my Mom at her gravesite, my thoughts became my words. "Mom, I want you to know that I love you. I regret and feel sad that I didn't' say or display that love as much as I should have, during our time together."

In our visits, Mom told me how proud she was of Tom and I to have gone to college, gotten our degree, and succeeded far beyond anything she'd imagined for us, as a young mother. When she related those words to me, I immediately let her know that she deserved all the credit, and I truly meant it!

Any success that my bother and I might have attained in our life is because of Violet Mildred Mae Lewis Axley, who gave us a "jump-start" toward a better life."

"Men Are What Their Mothers Made Them!"
Ralph Waldo Emerson...Poet

23

THE MYSTERY

So, what's the answer? That's what I keep asking myself.
What's it all about? Know what I mean?
Michael Caine...Alfie/1966 Movie

I vividly recall my introduction to religion and church at a very early age. I first attended an organized church in a small, one room, Pentecostal Church on a Sunday with my Grandma Box. I was about five years old as we walked into the church and sat down. The small congregation became quiet when a man dressed in "overalls" proceeded to the front of the church. I remember a lady that was standing near the man begin to lead everyone with a song before the preacher was to speak. After the Christian hymn, the man in overalls approached a lectern with his Bible. He looked over the small congregation for a minute or two and then, in a stern and somewhat angry voice, he said, "Everybody here is going to hell!"

In hearing those harsh words that day, fear and panic immediately shot up my spine. As a young child, the fear I felt made me react by sliding off the wooden church pew, where I sat next to my grandma, and run outside. Wherever "hell" was at that young age, I guess that I wasn't ready to go that day. Relating the story to others sounds kind of funny when I tell them about my experience, but that's how many of those "fire and brimstone" country preachers were in the late forties.

When I look back on how I fit into different beliefs over my lifetime, I can honestly say that I had been searching? In analyzing my "religious journey," I do know that I always wanted to be able to have that deep-rooted feeling in my heart of what I heard from other worshipers toward God and their belief system. But, as with many, religion has been puzzling to me? In my past half-hearted search for salvation, I've gone to Baptist churches, Methodist churches, Presbyterian Churches, Church of God, Nazarene, and countless others before being baptized as a Catholic.

I became Catholic when my sons were young because I felt I needed to try to understand and accept a religion, not just for me, but also for my family. My first wife and her family were devout Catholics. Even though we attended church regularly, and I had attended religious classes on Catholicism, I never really absorbed all of the theology. I still had questions on certain aspects, as I meandered my way through the teachings of the Church.

However, I am very happy I became a Catholic. Attending church with my family and then my sons being able to attend Catholic school made me feel that, maybe, I was doing the right thing for everyone.

I did, however, keep inquiring, reading, and learning about other theologies, over the years. As I thought about heaven, hell, sin, and where I might fit into different doctrines, I felt guilty that I couldn't finalize my beliefs.

Nowadays, religious education is abundant as people are a little more open-minded regarding some of their personal beliefs. Individuals are not just accepting church doctrine, pastoral opinions, or church dogma, as much as they did in years past. So, where am I today, regarding my beliefs?

I ran across a quote from the great Will Rogers, who was a cowboy, a famous actor, humorist, and a well-renowned journalist.

Will printed the following in an article on January 8, 1933.

"I was raised predominately a Methodist, but I have traveled so much…I don't know now just what I am. I know I have never been a non-believer. But, I can honestly tell you that I don't think that any one religion is "the religion!""

I've always wished I'd found the "one church," for me. As well, I've always felt somewhat jealous of those that had their divinity in life figured out. With much research and soul searching, I have nurtured my beliefs toward God, in which I've have come to realize that religion is about life and death. Life is to live and share the earthly experience of humanity and nature with love and gratitude, as we move toward the inevitable path toward an earthly end, which is Death!

As with Will Rogers, I don't think there is one way. Recently, I was watching a television show on PBS regarding the "Hubbell Telescope" sent into deep outer space. It showed the many millions of Galactic Stars, Planets, Black Holes, Nebula's, and beautiful images of the different "Universes." Our place in the Universe is "minute." A scientist may give you his thoughts about the Big Bang Theory, but truthfully, none of us know. It's left for each of us to decide what we believe, either for ourselves or with organized religion.

I believe there is a God or Creator. I can't help to believe in God when I see earth's nature and how things live, die, and are reborn every year. It's not an accident. I believe humans are part of God's nature.

I believe God created everything on this earth. I believe that there is a "hereafter, or heaven." I don't know if it's what people write about or whether St. Peter meets us at the golden gate or not, but I believe our spirit or soul lives on. Recalling my spiritual experience with my father when he passed, I always think of author and motivational speaker Dr. Stephen Covey's quote. "We Are Not Human Beings On A Spiritual Journey. We Are Spiritual Beings On A Human Journey."

Whether it's obeying the Ten Commandments or some other positive human doctrines, we should respect and honor our existence with others.

If someone would ask me about Jesus, I'd let him or her know that he was sent here from God, just as I believe all of us were sent here by our Creator. Jesus was spiritually enlightened to communicate God's love for us all. The message from Jesus was of "hope, forgiveness, and everlasting life." Whether it's through the lessons and principles we learn from chosen ones like Jesus, or other enlightened leaders and prophets of other faiths; I feel that religion is a way to individually, or as a community, tune in to that Universal God. I believe there is an afterlife. I believe that whether you go to church to tap into your goodness with others or worship individually to a higher power, your spirit will live on in eternity.

As the famous author, "Mark Twain" explained about the Mystery and how to cope with it, he wrote,

> *"To live is to be Courageous. The fear of death follows from the fear of life. A man who lives fully is prepared to die at any time."*
> *Be Courageous!*

EPILOGUE

I'M MOVIN ON, I'M LUCKY!

Every adversity, every failure, and every heartache, carries with it
the seed of an equal or greater benefit.
Napoleon Hill…Author

The year 2007 was a life changer. Having had a swollen lymph node that would not recede. After surgery, my doctor gave me the news that it was "Cancerous." Even though you know it beforehand, that bit of information made me focus and face the unwelcomed realization that I was not invincible.

I've told many of my friends that when you hear the three words, "You've Got Cancer," life instantly changes. You are now on a new journey!

After digesting the news and with the help of my son Tim, I had to plan my attack on how to beat the dreaded disease. When we researched whether to stay in Tulsa or go to a famed Cancer center for treatment, he said, "Dad, do you want the "A" team or the "B" team? We decided it was best to go to Houston.

At age sixty-three, and without going into all the details, I remember telling my son Tim, while at the famous MD Anderson Cancer

Center, that it was the first time I felt old. Feeling anxious and stressed, I had to reassess how I was going to recover?

My healing strategy was to always take the "next step" in my treatment and road to recovery. I seemed to have gone back to values that I'd learned in my athletic and business background, which was to confront a challenge by attacking it, no matter the circumstances. After we saw some of those who were fighting to live with Cancer at MD Anderson, we were in awe. I knew that I had to "step up" and do whatever it would take, both mentally and physically, as we watched how other patients fought for their lives, with grace.

After some very difficult Cancer treatments, I returned home from Houston. In recovery and while becoming very dependent on painkilling drugs, I started to have some self-doubts about my progress. But, sometimes, we need someone or something to trigger a change in attitude. As I was driving down a city toll road for a follow-up doctor's appointment and listening to the radio, a particular song caught my attention. In listening to the words, I started to personally identify with the inspiring message of letting go of your past and moving forward in your life. The lyrics of the song, "Movin On" by the group Rascal Flatts, was "my trigger," which help awaken me from my "self-pity." That evening, I quit pain killers "cold turkey." From that time on, I moved back into my competitive nature and looked forward to the next step of recovery. I was back to what I'd always done, which was to attack and to always, "Keep On, Keepin' On!"

In 2018 and after ten years, I was "Cancer Free." My battle with Cancer was a blessing! It helped me be more grateful for my life treasures and honor the simple things in life that I use to take for granted.

The old saying, "the harder you work, the luckier you are" is true for me. However, after I'd spent my whole life trying to make it, financially, I finally realized that my journey was not just about me, and making it. Life was about relationships. To be able to make friends throughout my life in school, business, and sports has been a blessing. I was lucky to have had the right mentors at crucial points in my life and smart enough to have been receptive of their advice and guidance.

I was also fortunate that I met and married my first wife, Carol, who partnered as we molded a family with two great sons. To be able to coach my sons and their friends from grade school through AAU basketball Championships was a gift. As a young father who had no real father of my own, I can honestly say that in raising my sons, I was "winging it." In looking back on those early years with my boys, I knew without a doubt that I would always be there for them.

Health is a life long process. At 74, I'm lucky that I'm still able to exercise and embrace my physical body, as well as stimulating my mind with new challenges.

I feel blessed that I had my brother Tom to share some unsettling adolescent years during our Mom's struggles, personally and financially. We were both lucky to have been there for each other to help take care of Mom toward the end of her life.

By chance, I was lucky that my wife, Stacey, came back into my life. I had been closed to relationships when, by luck, Stacey brought love back into my heart.

In assessing my journey, I'd say that my answer to Clint Eastwood when he asks the question in the movie, Dirty Harry… "Do you feel lucky, Punk?"

Yes, Absolutely!

From left to right, Sarah, Edith, Cecil, and Arthur Axley. My Grandpa Axley, whom I'd never known, died in 1936. Grandma Axley Box was left with four children, and they all had to work on the farms in Bixby to survive.

Arthur Allen Axley before marriage to Rosie.

Arthur Axley and Rosa Kingston Axley.

A hand water pump that was outside the kitchen door. We pumped fresh drinking water to be carried into "The Shack" by bucket.

Icebox that we used in "The Shack." 25 lbs. of ice was placed in the top with items that needed to be cooled placed in the bottom. Even year's later; people called a refrigerator an "Icebox."

Outdoor toilet. This is where everyone "did their business." On Halloween, many mischievous teens would turn over the toilets, as a prank.

Grandma Rosie was remarried to William (Bill) Box and had one child. Jodean is shown in Grandma's lap. Top Row (left to right) are the Axley's. My Aunt Sarah, Uncle Art, my father Cecil, and Edith

My Uncle Art Axley (left), became a very successful funeral homeowner. Cecil Axley (right), my father, was homeless when he passed away at age sixty-three, of unknown circumstances.

My brother, Tommy (right), and I played baseball in Tulsa, one summer, while attending school in the small town of Leonard, Ok. When we moved to the "Westside" of Tulsa, I played for the Red Fork Lions, and Tom played for Park Elementary.

Coaching young men was what Oklahoma Hall of Fame coach Bill Allen did best. He was my high school basketball coach and life long mentor.

Building a new program at Mason High School was a challenge and a pleasure. I was in business for forty years, but coaching is still in my blood.

My time as a 1966 Oklahoma Sooner has a special place in my heart. I have many cherished memories of my teammates, and still, have a bond with many of them at the annual OU Basketball Alumni functions.

Then & Now. Joe Bogan (right), my "roomie" at OU, as players, and at a recent 2019 OU basketball game.

Jostens December 1975 New Man Training School. I'm Lower Right.

MTM Award Presentation. Steve & Tim Axley, front row. (right)

Mom's education journey was from the first through the eighth grade. (below). As a young woman, (above) she was fun and gregarious. She kept her keen sense of humor throughout her life. My brother and I teased Mom about her belief in extraterrestrials and, especially, the zodiac signs to determine the best time to play the slots.

My brother Tom with Mom, and me.

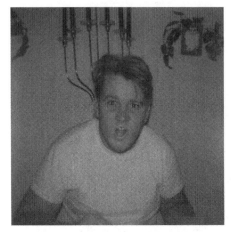

My man Freddie, as a young man, doing what he does best, which is being Freddie!

Freddie and I, reminiscing over dinner at Ruth's Chris Steakhouse in Tulsa, Oklahoma 2019.

Mike Pounds and I at the annual Big 12 basketball tournament. Mike is an Oklahoma State Cowboy fan, and I'm totally all OU, "Boomer Sooner!"

My two sons, Tim (left) and Steve, (right). I'm a proud father!

My lovely wife Stacey, and our pride and joy, Lulu!

Coaching my sons and outstanding players while winning national BCI championships in 1987 and 1989 with the Tulsa Hawks was a highlight.

Dr. John Bryan (center) was the backbone of our Tulsa Hawks team. He and Car-
los Gripado (left) were instrumental in initiating the elite AAU high school basketball competition in Tulsa and Eastern Oklahoma, which led to numerous championships. I was fortunate to be able to coach with them.

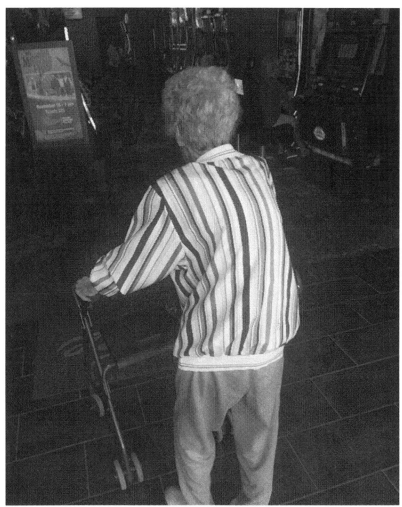

Mom's adolescent years were during the great depression. Later, she raised two boys as, mostly, a single mom. In her senior years, even though she was very ill, she still wanted to participate in life. She loved getting out and going to the casino. The picture above is the epitome of her willingness to try to stay active. At age 89, she's headed to her perch at the slots to…

Keep On, Keepin' On!

Made in the USA
Lexington, KY
23 September 2019